Our Catholic Faith

A Summary of Basic Beliefs

Rev. Msgr. John F. Barry

Official Theological Consultant
Rev. Edward K. Braxton, Ph.D., S.T.D.

Curriculum Consultant
Elinor R. Ford

Sadlier
A Division of
William H. Sadlier, Inc.
New York
Chicago
Los Angeles

Nihil Obstat
Reverend James J. Uppena
Censor Deputatus

Imprimatur
✠ Most Reverend Cletus F.
O'Donnell
Bishop of Madison
February 13, 1987

Excerpts from Good News Bible
copyright © American Bible
Society 1966, 1971, 1976.

Excerpts from the English
translation of *Rite of Marriage* ©
1969, International Committee on
English in the Liturgy, Inc.
(ICEL); excerpts from the English
translation of *Rite of Baptism for
Children* © 1969, ICEL; excerpts
from the English translation of
Lectionary for Mass © 1969,
ICEL; excerpts from the English
translation of *The Roman Missal*
© 1973, ICEL; excerpts from the
English translation of *Rite of
Penance* © 1974, ICEL; excerpts
from the English translation of
*Ordination of Deacons, Priests,
and Bishops* © 1975, ICEL;
excerpts from the English
translation of *Pastoral Care of
the Sick: Rites of Anointing and
Viaticum* © 1982, ICEL. All rights
reserved.

Art Director
Grace Kao

Illustrations by
Creative Communicators, Inc.

Photo acknowledgements appear
on page 112.

William H. Sadlier, Inc.
11 Park Place
New York, New York 10007
ISBN: 0-8215-2195-0
23456789/987

Dear Student:

This book, *Our Catholic Faith,* is written to help you learn
more about your Catholic faith. It reviews the main ideas
of your faith. Once you understand these, you will be better
able to live your life as a Catholic who loves and follows Jesus.
You will also be prepared to continue your study of the faith.

To make the best use of this book:

- Listen attentively as your teacher explains each chapter.

- Share your feelings, your ideas, and your thoughts
  about what is written in the chapter.

- In your own words explain the main ideas in each
  chapter. (These are usually summarized in colored frames
  at the beginning of each new topic.)

- Memorize the main ideas in each chapter.

- Think about how you can do what each chapter is asking
  you to do. Make a promise to try to live your faith a
  little better each day. Pray to Jesus and His Mother,
  Mary, for the strength to keep your promise, or to have
  the courage to try again when you fail.

Do know that all who wrote this book for you, and those
who teach it, love you very much. We want you to come
to know God, Jesus, and His Mother better so that you,
too, will know how to keep them with you in times of joy,
of worry, and of sadness. Ask your teacher, your parent,
your priest, or a friend to sign this page with you as their
promise to help you learn and live *Our Catholic Faith.*

_____

Your Name

_____

Your Parent/Teacher/Priest/Friend who will help you

Contents

Unit I   We Are Created and Saved

1. God Is Our Creator — 6
(Creation, Original Sin, Promise of a Savior)

2. Jesus Comes to Us — 12
(Incarnation, Good News, Kingdom of God)

3. Jesus Is Our Savior — 18
(Passion, Death, Resurrection)

Unit I Test — 24

Unit II   We Are Followers of Jesus

4. Jesus Sends the Holy Spirit — 26
(Promise of the Spirit, Pentecost, Early Church)

5. The Catholic Church Today — 32
(Worship and Service, Marks of the Church,
Pope and Bishops)

6. The Seven Sacraments — 38
(Jesus and Signs, Seven Sacraments, Life-Giving Signs)

Unit II Test — 44

First Semester Test — 46

Unit III   We Belong to the Catholic Church

7. Becoming Catholic — 48
(Baptism, Grace and Original Sin, Confirmation)

8. The Sacrament of the Eucharist — 54
(Jesus' Gift of Himself, Celebrating Eucharist,
Union with Christ)

9. The Mass — 60
(Liturgy of the Word, Liturgy of the Eucharist,
Service of Others)

Unit III Test — 66

Unit IV We Live As Catholics

10. The Ten Commandments 68
(Laws of God, Love of God,
Love of Neighbor)

11. The Beatitudes 74
(Jesus' Teaching, Guidelines for True
Happiness, Faith, Hope, and Love)

12. The Sacrament of Reconciliation 80
(Sin, Temptation, Formation and Examination of
Conscience, Celebrating the Sacrament)

13. Living as Good Catholics 86
(Last Judgment, Corporal Works,
Spiritual Works)

14. Mary and the Saints 92
(Mary, Rosary, Saints)

Unit IV Test 98

Second Semester Test 100

A Review of the Year 102

The Liturgical Year 104

Prayers 106

Glossary 107

Things to Know 109

Index 110

Certificate of Achievement 112

Sacrament of Reconciliation Inside Back Cover

1 God Is Our Creator

Faith Words

Creator:
a name for God who created or made our universe and everything in it.

original sin:
the sin of the first human beings in which we all share.

God Is Our Creator

When we look at a brilliant
rainbow splashed across the summer sky . . .

Or hear the pounding of the waves
against the shoreline.. . .

Or smell the flowers,
or hear a robin sing . . .

Or touch the new softness
of a baby's hand . . .

When we stand in awe before
the stars that light our universe . . .

**We praise and thank our God who
made them all!!**

What have you seen today that reminds you of God? Describe what you saw in words or through art.

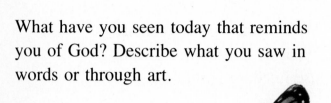

We Will Learn

1 God created the whole universe.

2 People turned away from God.

3 God promised to send a Savior.

1 God created the whole universe.

From the Bible, the holy book of God's story, we learn that everything in the universe was created by God.

After God had created all things, God made human beings.

The Bible tells us: "God created people in God's image . . . male and female God created them" (from Genesis 1:26–27).

The Bible calls the first man and woman whom God made Adam and Eve. God gave Adam and Eve charge over creation and trusted them to care for it all— the animals, flowers, trees, fishes, even the running rivers and the deep oceans. All of creation was theirs to enjoy and protect. God wanted people to love and to be happy in the beautiful world God had made.

The whole story of creation is found in Genesis 1:1—2:4.

Name some of the things God created.
Who is supposed to care for God's world? Why?

The Bible story tells us that Adam and Eve did not live up to God's trust. They did not use their freedom wisely. They chose to act selfishly and to turn away from the loving God who had created them. When they chose to turn away from God, they sinned. This first sin is called *original sin*.

What is the first sin called? What do you think it means to use freedom wisely?

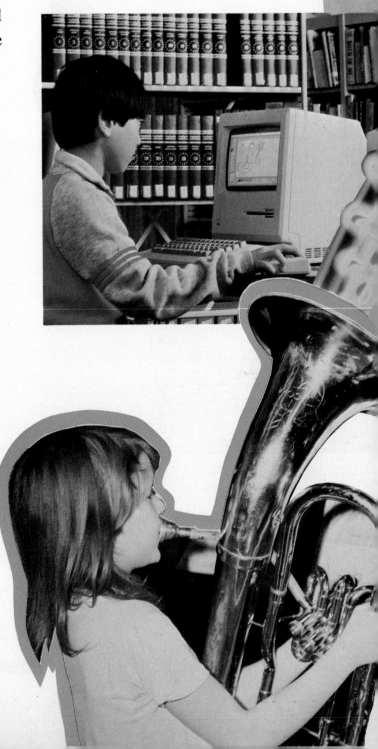

2 People turned away from God.

God created a world where people would live in peace and joy. In God's plan, human beings would never be sick or die. They were created to be happy with God forever. That was God's plan for human beings.

God gave the first human beings many wonderful gifts.

- They could feel and love.
- They could think and wonder.
- They could create and explore.
- They could ask questions and seek answers.
- They could choose and decide.

One of God's greatest gifts to Adam and Eve was the gift of freedom. From the very beginning, they were free to choose either to do good or to do evil. God would not force them to do anything. God trusted them to act out of love rather than selfishness.

Do You Know

Do you know where we find the story of creation?

It comes from the *Bible* (Genesis 1—3). The Bible is the most important book of all for God's people because it is God's Word. It tells the story of how God created us, loved us, and came among us.

The Bible helps us to learn about who God is and how we have become God's own people.

9

3 God promised to send a Savior.

Even though Adam and Eve sinned, God still loved them. God had a marvelous plan. God would send a Savior, God's only Son, Jesus Christ. Jesus would save all of us from sin, selfishness, and death. He would show us how to love God and one another.

Because God has given us the great gift of Jesus to be our Savior, we can know how God wants us to live. We can live now as friends of Jesus and be happy with God forever in heaven.

What was God's plan to save us?

How can you show your love for God?

I Have Learned

Fill in the correct words.

God created people to be

_____ with God forever.

Adam and Eve turned away from God. They chose to

_____

God promised to send a

_____

I Will Do

Name some of the gifts God has given us.

Which one of these do you think is God's greatest gift to you?

How do you use this gift?
What will you do to praise and thank God for this gift?

Prayer

Prayer is talking and listening to God. We can pray to thank God and to praise God. We can ask God for what we need. Here is a prayer praising God.

I will praise you, Lord,
    with all my heart;
I will tell of all the wonderful
    things you have done!

Psalm 9:1

Remember

God created and loved human beings even though they sinned.

God promised to send a Savior, Jesus Christ, to save all people from sin, selfishness, and death.

Review

1. What did God want people to do with the world God had created?

2. What does the Bible tell us Adam and Eve chose to do?

3. Who is the Savior?

4. How does it make you feel to know that a loving God created and saved the world?

Family Note

In this lesson, your child learned that our loving God created all things and that, in spite of people's sin, God sent Jesus Christ to save us. Help your child to review the lesson by discussing the *Remember* and *Review* on this page.

Faith Words

Incarnation:
> God's Son becoming a member of our human family.

Gospel:
> the good news of God's love for us.

Kingdom of God:
> the power of God's love in the hearts and lives of all people.

Being Alive!

Each picture shows something all human beings do. From the list, select the words that you think best fit each picture. Write them on the line.

Things We Do

We love.

We grow.

We share.

We feel afraid.

We laugh.

We have friends.

We think.

We understand.

We question.

We play.

We cry.

We learn.

All of these things tell us something about what it means to be human.

Which of these things are most important to you now? Why?

We Will Learn

1 Jesus Christ, the Son of God, was born into our human family.

2 The Gospel tells us how good Jesus was to everyone.

3 Jesus preached about the Kingdom of God.

1 Jesus Christ, the Son of God, was born into our human family.

Jesus Christ, God's only Son became human like us. He shared the same human experiences that we all have. He was like us in every way except that He never sinned.

The Bible tells us that one day the angel Gabriel brought a message to a Jewish girl named Mary. Gabriel told her that God wanted her to be the mother of God's Son, Jesus. She did not understand how this could happen, but she believed and trusted in God.

Mary said yes to God's message. "I am the Lord's servant," said Mary. "May it happen to me as you have said" (from Luke 1:26–37).

This event is called the *Annunciation*. God's promise to send us a Savior was about to be fulfilled.

We celebrate the birth of Jesus on December 25, the feast of Christmas. Jesus, God's own Son, became one of us. He became a member of the human family. This coming of God's Son into the world is called the *Incarnation*.

What do we mean by the Incarnation?

What does it mean to you that Jesus became a member of the human family?

Do You Know

Each Sunday at Mass we hear a gospel reading from the Bible. The priest or deacon reads to us from the Gospel according to Matthew, Mark, Luke, or John.

2 The Gospel tells us how good Jesus was to everyone.

Jesus taught people through His words and actions to know and love God. The good things that Jesus did while He was on earth are described in the part of the Bible we call the four Gospels. The word *gospel* itself means "good news." One of the Gospels tells us, "He healed many people from their sicknesses, diseases, and evil spirits, and gave sight to many people" (from Luke 7:21).

The good news of Jesus is that God loves, forgives, and cares for all of us. No one is left out.

The Gospels tell us how Jesus taught us to love others as God loves us. Jesus did this by:

- feeding the hungry,
- teaching the ignorant,
- curing the sick,
- forgiving sinners,
- being a friend to the poor,
- urging people to love God and one another more.

Jesus called people to follow Him and share His work and teaching. "Come, follow Me," He said (Mark 10:21).

Jesus asked twelve of His friends to be leaders of those who followed Him. We call them *Apostles*. He placed Saint Peter at their head. Jesus promised Peter: "You are a rock, and on this rock foundation I will build my Church" (Matthew 16:18). The *Church* is the community Jesus founded.

What do the Gospels tell us about the ways Jesus was good to everyone?

Name one way you can follow Jesus today.

3 Jesus preached about the Kingdom of God.

Jesus is the Savior—the one God promised to send to save the world. When Jesus began His preaching, He told the people that He had been sent by God to bring the Good News of God's Kingdom to all people. The Kingdom of God means the power of God's love in the hearts and lives of all people.

Jesus told people that they must be sorry for their sins. He said they must turn away from doing evil and do the good things God asks. When people do these good things, they share in God's Kingdom.

We do what God asks of us when we try to love others and be fair to everyone. When we live this way we show others that God's Kingdom is a Kingdom of peace, justice, and love. God wants all of us to be happy now and forever in the Kingdom of God.

What did Jesus mean by the Kingdom of God?

What must we do to share in God's Kingdom?

I Have Learned

Match the words in Column A with the correct description in Column B. Write the number of the word next to the correct description.

Column A	Column B
1. Annunciation	___ God's Son becoming a member of our human family
2. Gospel	
3. Incarnation	___ rule of God's love in our hearts and lives
4. Kingdom of God	___ good news of God's love
	___ message of the angel to Mary

Prayer

It is good to ask God for the things that we need and for the help that only God can give us. Here is a prayer asking for God's help.

Jesus, God's own Son,
help us to do good for everyone
as You did. Show us how to
work for God's Kingdom in all
we do and say. Amen.

I Will Do

Here are some things I could do to work for God's Kingdom.

- Love others.
- Be fair.
- Live in peace.
- Make others happy.

Choose one of the above that you could do today or tomorrow.

Explain how you could do it. Most of all, will you really do it?

Remember

Jesus Christ became one of us to show us how to live as members of God's Kingdom.

The Gospels tell us how good Jesus was to everyone.

Jesus is our Savior and shares with us the promise of the Kingdom of God.

Review

1. What is the Incarnation?

2. What is the Good News of Jesus?

3. Name ways you can share in the Kingdom of God.

4. How does it feel to know we have a Savior who knows how it feels to be human?

Family Note

The focus of this lesson was that Jesus Christ, the Son of God, was born into our human family and that He preached about the Kingdom of God. Discuss with your child ways that we can all, in our everyday lives, work for God's Kingdom. Close by praying together the prayer of this lesson.

Faith Words

Holy Thursday:
the day Jesus gave us the Eucharist at the Last Supper.

Good Friday:
the day Jesus died.

Easter Sunday:
the day Jesus rose from the dead. This event is called the resurrection.

New Life

"It's a girl! She's fine, and she's beautiful," shouted Dr. Jason through his surgical mask. He held up the newborn child for her happy parents to see.

As the doctor went to check on his other patients, he thought of that moment when he showed the baby to her parents.

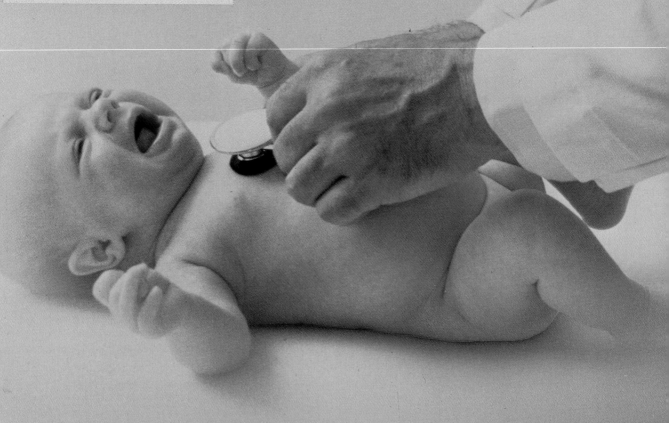

Even though he had brought hundreds of babies into this world, that moment still thrilled him— seeing a new life at the instant of birth. It still seemed like a miracle to him.

Dr. Jason's last stop was to visit a friend. Mr. Gregg was an elderly gentleman who was dying. Dr. Jason believed his friend would not live through the night. He stayed with the old man for a long time, making him as comfortable as possible. Suddenly Mr. Gregg opened his eyes. He smiled at Dr. Jason. Then he died.

That night, Dr. Jason could not sleep. He kept thinking of the baby that was born. Then he thought about the smile on his dying friend's face.

He kept hearing the words ''new life.'' Finally, Dr. Jason realized why. On this one day, he had helped a baby be born to new life. He had also helped a friend prepare for death and for the new life that was to come after death.

Dr. Jason felt blessed. He had seen what new life was all about.

Have you ever held a new baby? How did it make you feel?

What do the words ''new life'' mean to you?

Has someone you loved died? How did you feel? Do you think that person is gone forever?

What does it mean to live forever?

We Will Learn

1 On Holy Thursday, at the Last Supper, Jesus gave us the Eucharist.

2 On Good Friday, Jesus died on the cross.

3 On Easter Sunday, Jesus rose from the dead.

1 On Holy Thursday, at the Last Supper, Jesus gave us the Eucharist.

Jesus loved us so much that He was willing to die for us. The day before Jesus died is called Holy Thursday. On the evening of Holy Thursday Jesus gathered with His friends for a Last Supper. Jesus knew that His friends would need help to live as His followers after His death. So, during the special meal, Jesus took the bread and wine and changed them into His Body and Blood.

Jesus gave to some of His followers, the Apostles, the power to change bread and wine into His Body and Blood. Jesus would be with His friends in a special way whenever they came together for this meal which is called the *Eucharist*. Receiving Jesus' Body and Blood in the Eucharist would strengthen them and help them to live as His followers.

What did Jesus do on Holy Thursday?

Imagine you are at the Last Supper, how do you feel?

Do You Know

Each year on Good Friday we remember that Jesus loved us so much that He was willing to suffer and die for us. In our homes and churches, we have crosses with the figure of Jesus on them. We call these *crucifixes*. They remind us that Jesus died for us. He is our Savior.

2 On Good Friday, Jesus died on the cross.

Jesus was condemned to death because He claimed to be God's Son. After beating Him and making fun of Him the soldiers put a crown of thorns on Jesus' head. The soldiers forced Jesus to carry a heavy cross to Calvary, a hill outside Jerusalem. Most of Jesus' friends ran away and hid. They were afraid that they also would be arrested and have to suffer as Jesus did. Jesus our Savior was nailed to a cross and left to die. He was crucified.

While Jesus was nailed to the cross, He forgave those who had crucified Him. He prayed: "Father, forgive them, they do not know what they are doing" (from Luke 23:34).

Jesus had often told His friends to forgive their enemies. Now, by His own example, He showed them how.

Why did Jesus' friends run away?

Have you ever found it hard to be a loyal friend? Tell about it.

Have you ever forgiven someone who treated you unfairly? Tell about it.

3 On Easter Sunday, Jesus rose from the dead.

On Easter Sunday morning, some women went to the tomb where Jesus had been buried. It was empty! They thought someone had stolen Jesus' body. But soon Jesus Himself appeared to Mary Magdalene and a little later to a group of His followers. They were filled with excitement and joy. Jesus was alive!

God raised Jesus to new life. Jesus saved us from sin and death. We believe the promise of Jesus that death will not be the end for us.

We, too, will be born into new life when we die. We will live forever with God.

We call Jesus' rising to new life after death His *resurrection*. Each year we celebrate our Savior's dying and rising from the dead during Holy Thursday, Good Friday, Holy Saturday, and Easter Sunday. We celebrate that Jesus Christ has risen to new life and that we, too, will live a new life forever with God. All of these days are part of one great time of prayer in our Church. We call this time *Holy Week*. It is the time from Palm Sunday to Easter.

What happened on Easter Sunday?

Why do we believe that we will be born into new life when we die?

I Have Learned

Complete the following.

On _____ _____ Jesus changed bread and wine into His

_____ and _____ .

On _____ _____ , Jesus died

on the _____ .

On _____ _____ , Jesus rose from the dead.

We call Jesus' rising to new life

after death the _____

What does "new life" mean to you now?

What do you think it will be like to live with God forever?

I Will Do

Each Sunday when we celebrate the Eucharist, we remember that Jesus died for us and rose from the dead.

How will you try to remember this the next time you go to church?

Prayer

The Church often gives us words to use when we pray. When we pray together as members of God's family, we use the prayers of the Church. Here is a prayer we pray on Good Friday.

We adore You, O Christ, and we bless You, because by Your Holy Cross You have redeemed the world. Amen.

Remember

On Holy Thursday at the Last Supper, Jesus gave us the Eucharist.

Jesus died on the cross on Good Friday and rose from the dead on Easter Sunday.

Review

1. What did Jesus do at the Last Supper?

2. Why did Jesus die?

3. What do we call the day He rose from the dead?

4. What do you think about new life after death?

Family Note

The focus of this lesson was on Jesus' giving us the Eucharist, and His sacrificial death and rising to new life. Use the *Faith Words* to help review with your child what he or she studied in this lesson.

Unit I Test

Write the word from this word list that best fits each numbered definition. One is done for you.

Kingdom of God   original sin
Creator   Holy Thursday
Good Friday   Incarnation
Gospel   Easter
Bible   crucifix

1. The Good News of God's love for us

   _____ Gospel _____

2. A name for God who made our universe and everything in it

   _____

3. The sin of the first human beings in which we all share

   _____

4. The day Jesus gave us the Eucharist

   _____

5. The power of God's love in our hearts and lives

   _____

6. A cross with a figure of Jesus on it

   _____

7. The day Jesus rose from the dead

   _____

8. The holy book of God's story

   _____

9. God's Son becoming a member of our human family

   _____

10. The day Jesus died

    _____

Put the Biblical events in the order in which they happened, using numbers 1 through 10. One is done for you.

11. _____ Adam and Eve turned away from God.

12. _____ Mary said yes to God's message.

13. _____ Jesus rose from the dead on Easter Sunday.

14. _____ Jesus, God's own Son, became a member of the human family on December 25.

15. _____ Jesus forgave those who crucified Him.

16. _____ God gave Adam and Eve charge over creation.

17. _____ Jesus asked twelve of His friends to be Apostles, leaders, of those who followed Him.

18. _____ Jesus died on Good Friday.

19. _____ The angel Gabriel brought a message from God to Mary.

20. _____ At the Last Supper on Holy Thursday, Jesus gave us the Eucharist.

From the list of words below, write in the word or phrase that best completes each sentence.

die	people	God's Kingdom
world	joy	one of us
live	peace	new life

21. God created _____ in God's image.

22. God created a _____ where people would live in _____ and _____ .

23. Jesus promised that we will be born to _____ _____ when we _____ .

24. Jesus Christ became _____ _____ _____ to show us how to _____ as members of _____ _____ .

25. Think first. Then answer this question. What is the good news of Jesus? What does it mean to you?

_____

_____

_____

Faith Words

Blessed Trinity:
the three divine Persons in one God, the Father, the Son, and the Holy Spirit.

Church:
the community of the baptized followers of Jesus Christ.

Holy Spirit:
God, the Third Person of the Blessed Trinity.

A Call for Help

Some years ago a young man, poor and discouraged, stopped by his church to pray. The young man wanted to be a comedian, to make people laugh, to bring the joy of good humor to the lives of others. But the young man could not get a job—he was an unknown, and no one would hire him. That night he prayed to St. Jude. He asked for help to get started in the career that he knew was right for him. His name was Danny Thomas.

Danny Thomas went on to become a well-loved and successful performer in movies and on television. In gratitude to St. Jude, he built a fine children's hospital named for the saint. And today Danny Thomas is still helping others by appearing at benefits for charitable causes and helping others in many other ways.

Indeed on that long-ago night, Danny Thomas's cry for help was heard. And he has returned that gift, over and over, to his fellow human beings.

Have you ever received help when you really needed it? Tell about it.

What do you do when you need help?

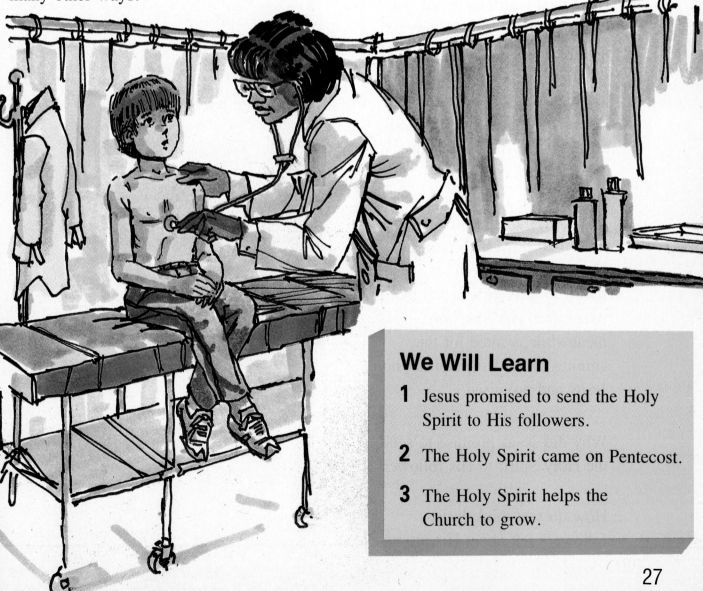

We Will Learn

1 Jesus promised to send the Holy Spirit to His followers.

2 The Holy Spirit came on Pentecost.

3 The Holy Spirit helps the Church to grow.

1 Jesus promised to send the Holy Spirit to His followers.

2 The Holy Spirit came on Pentecost.

Jesus knew people would need help to live as He had asked them. The night before Jesus died, He promised to send them another Helper, the Holy Spirit, who would stay with them forever. The Holy Spirit would teach them and help them remember all Jesus told them (from John 14:16,26).

After Jesus rose from the dead, He stayed with His friends for a while, teaching and helping them. He told them to bring the good news of God's love to all the world. Jesus said, ''Remember, I will be with you always, until the end of time'' (Matthew 28:19-20).

Forty days after Easter, Jesus left His followers to return to His Father in heaven. Jesus' return to heaven is called the *Ascension*. His followers, meanwhile, waited for the coming of the Holy Spirit whom Jesus had promised.

Why did Jesus promise to send the Holy Spirit to His followers?

How do you think Jesus' followers felt about His promise?

On the Jewish feast of Pentecost, the followers of Jesus were together praying and waiting for the Holy Spirit. As they prayed, something astounding happened.

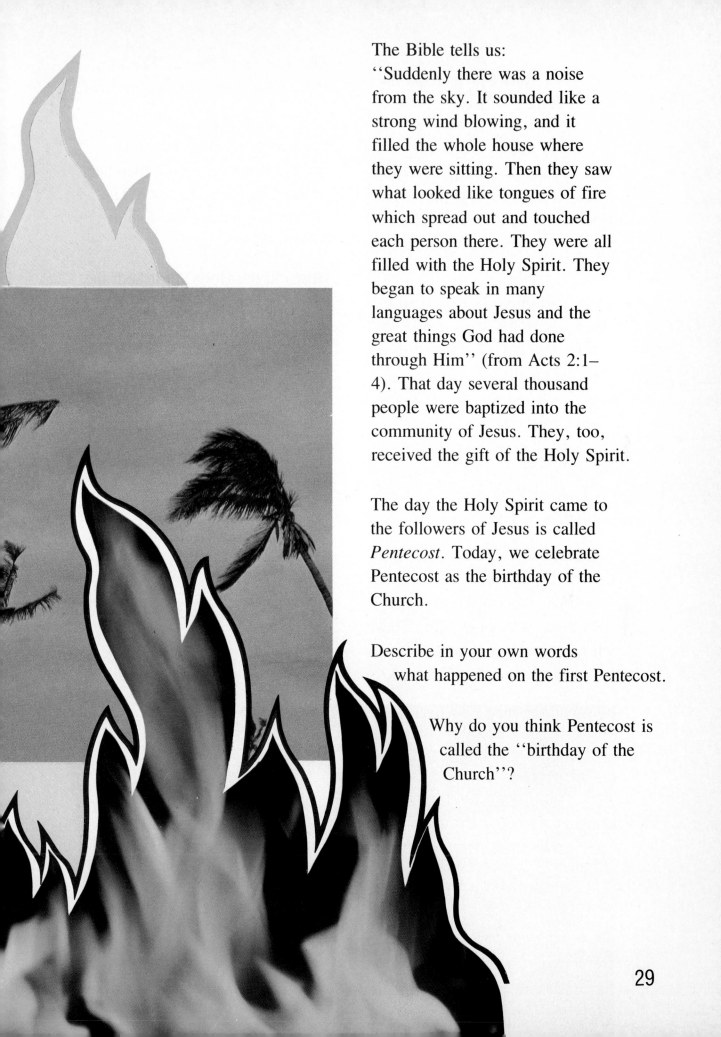

The Bible tells us:
"Suddenly there was a noise from the sky. It sounded like a strong wind blowing, and it filled the whole house where they were sitting. Then they saw what looked like tongues of fire which spread out and touched each person there. They were all filled with the Holy Spirit. They began to speak in many languages about Jesus and the great things God had done through Him" (from Acts 2:1–4). That day several thousand people were baptized into the community of Jesus. They, too, received the gift of the Holy Spirit.

The day the Holy Spirit came to the followers of Jesus is called *Pentecost*. Today, we celebrate Pentecost as the birthday of the Church.

Describe in your own words what happened on the first Pentecost.

Why do you think Pentecost is called the "birthday of the Church"?

29

3 The Holy Spirit helps the Church to grow.

Pentecost was the beginning of a new life for the little group of Jesus' followers. The Holy Spirit filled them with courage and love and helped them to share the good news of Jesus with everyone.

More and more people asked to be baptized. They wanted to follow Jesus and to be part of His community, the Church. They gathered together to pray and to celebrate the Eucharist in memory of Jesus Christ. People began to call His followers "Christians" because they were followers of Jesus Christ.

The early Christians tried to live the way Jesus taught. Those who were rich shared what they had with those who were poor. Those who were well took care of those who were sick or handicapped.

People said of them, "See how these Christians love one another!"

The Church continues to grow. Each of us receives the Holy Spirit when we become members of the Church at Baptism. The Holy Spirit helps us to live as followers of Jesus.

How did the Holy Spirit help the early Church?

How would you like the Holy Spirit to help you?

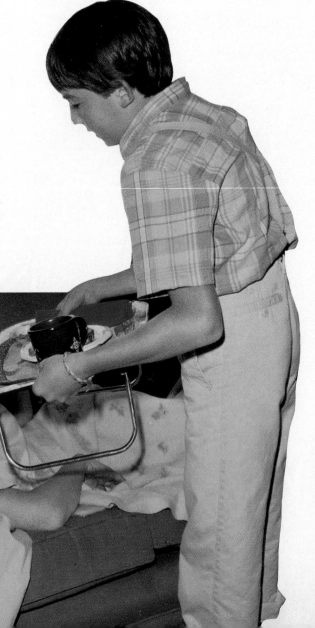

I Have Learned

Reread the Bible story of the first Pentecost in Acts of the Apostles 2:1–11. Tell the story of what happened as if you were there.

Imagine yourself telling a friend about God's love for people, as shown on the first Pentecost. What would you say?

I Will Do

Think about the story you have told. What one thing will you do this week to show you are happy to be a part of the Church?

Prayer

The Church invites us to begin our prayer with the Sign of the Cross. We make the Sign of the Cross by placing our right hand on our forehead, chest, and on each shoulder while saying the following prayer.

In the name of the Father, and of the Son, and of the Holy Spirit, Amen.

Come, Holy Spirit, fill our hearts with the fire of Your love. Amen.

Remember

Jesus promised to send His followers the Holy Spirit.

The Holy Spirit came to the followers of Jesus on Pentecost.

The Holy Spirit helped the early Church to grow in love and service to others.

Review

1. Why did Jesus promise to send the Holy Spirit to His followers?

2. When did the Holy Spirit come to the followers of Jesus?

3. How did the Holy Spirit change the followers of Jesus?

4. How might the Holy Spirit help you to change?

Family Note

This lesson focused on Jesus' promise of the Spirit, Pentecost, and the growth of the early Church. Review with your child the story of the first Pentecost, and then let your child share his or her story from the *I Have Learned* activity.

5 The Catholic Church Today

Faith Words

pope:
> the successor of St. Peter who leads and serves the whole Church.

bishops:
> the successors of the Apostles.

worship:
> to praise and honor God.

Every Sunday Morning

Jerry sat at the window, looking at the Catholic church across the street. Jerry was not a Catholic, but he liked to get up early on Sunday mornings and watch the neighborhood come slowly to life. The rest of his family were still sleeping.

Jerry had noticed the same scenes unfold every Sunday morning since they moved here. Every few hours the church bells would ring, and then people started to come. They came by car or bus or on foot, ones or twos or whole families. Some boys and girls came on bikes, one or two wearing school jackets. Some of the older people carried canes or clung to one another's arms for fear of falling.

What, Jerry wondered, brought them to this church. A new group came every few hours till well after noon. What did they find there that made getting up and out so worthwhile for them?

Jerry wondered whom he could ask.

How would you answer Jerry's questions?

If you took Jerry to your church, what would you point out to him first?

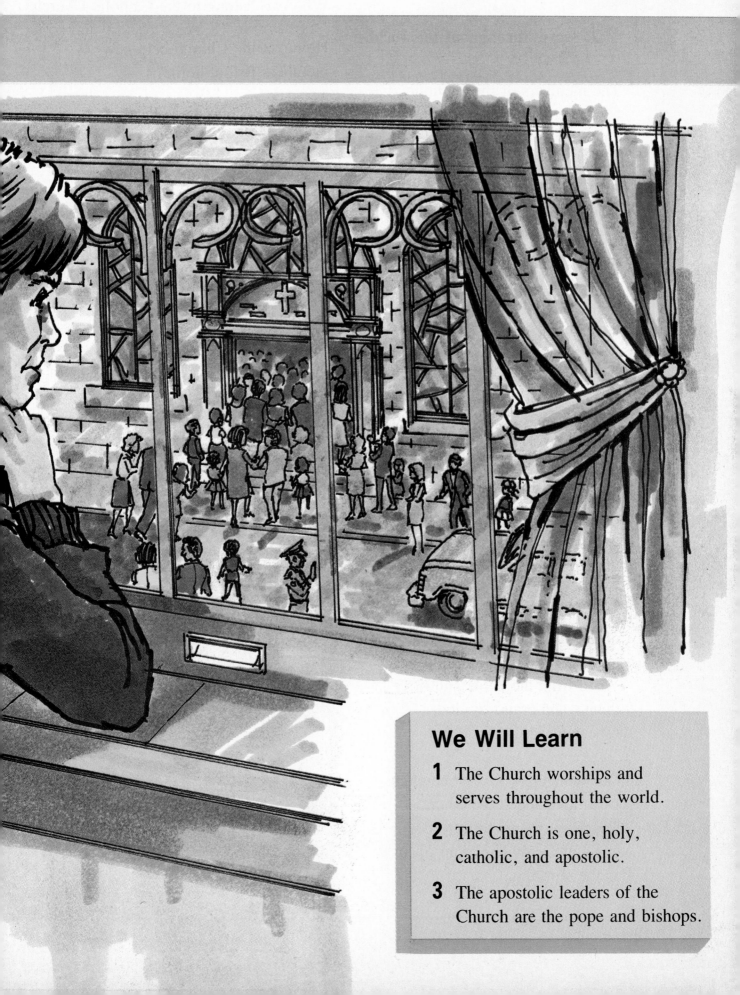

We Will Learn

1 The Church worships and serves throughout the world.

2 The Church is one, holy, catholic, and apostolic.

3 The apostolic leaders of the Church are the pope and bishops.

1 The Church worships and serves throughout the world.

The members of the Catholic Church gather to worship in churches all over the world.

In our churches, we are surrounded by reminders of God and the things of God. Statues of Jesus, Mary, Joseph, and the saints, burning candles, pictures, Stations of the Cross—all these are reminders of our fellowship with holy people and holy things. They remind us that Jesus is truly present with us in our churches.

No one is excluded from belonging to the Catholic Church. Men, women, old people and children, members of all nationalities and races, people who speak different languages—all are welcome. All of us gather to pray to God together. We listen to God's Word from the Bible and offer thanks and praise to God, especially in the Eucharist.

Our worship of God strengthens us to love and serve others. Together, we go forth to be signs of God's Kingdom of love in the world.

Who can belong to the Catholic Church?

How can the Church help new members feel at home?

What might you do to help?

Do You Know

In the Church others who are not ordained also help carry on the work that Jesus gave to Peter and the Apostles. Lay people and Religious Brothers and Sisters share in the work of the Church, teaching and serving as Jesus did.

2 The Church is one, holy, catholic, and apostolic.

The Holy Spirit helped the early Church to love and serve others. The Holy Spirit continues to help the Church today.

We are members of the Catholic Church. As Catholics, we have four special words that help us to understand the Church. We call these the *marks* of the Church. We say that the Church is *one*, *holy*, *catholic*, and *apostolic*. We believe that the Church is *one*. We have one God, one Savior, one Gospel, and one Spirit who guides us.

The Church is *holy*. This means that through the Church the grace of God comes to all the world. The Church shares with all people the holiness of Jesus.

The Church is *catholic*, which means open to all. As Catholics, we believe that all people are invited to be followers of Jesus. No one is left out. The Church is for all people, everywhere.

As Catholics, we believe that the Church is *apostolic*. This means that our pope and bishops, as the ordained successors of the Apostles, continue the work started by Jesus.

In your own words, tell what the words *one*, *holy*, *catholic* and *apostolic* mean to you.

What can you do to show you are proud to belong to the Catholic Church?

35

3 The apostolic leaders of the Church are the pope and bishops.

Jesus named Peter to be the first pope. He wanted Peter and the other Apostles, who were the first bishops, to teach others all that He had taught them.

Our pope and bishops today who follow in the steps of Peter and the Apostles are called the *successors* to the Apostles. This means that with the help of the Holy Spirit, they teach, serve, and lead the Church as Peter and the Apostles did.

Our Holy Father the Pope is the successor of St. Peter and the leader of the whole Catholic Church.

What is the name of our pope?

Bishops are the successors of the Apostles. Today most bishops teach, serve, and lead large parts of the Church called *dioceses*.

Name your diocese.
Name your bishop.

Priests and deacons are ordained ministers of the Church who teach, serve, and lead in our *parishes*.

Name your parish.
Name your pastor and the other priests and deacons in your parish.

Each of us helps our pope, bishops, and priests by learning and living our faith.

Prayer

Sometimes we pray prayers from the Bible. Here is one of them.

I love the house where you live, O Lord, the place where your glory dwells.

Psalm 26:8

I Have Learned

Match the words in Column A with the correct description in Column B. Write the number of the word next to the correct description.

Column A   **Column B**

1. catholic   ___ is the successor of St. Peter

2. pope   ___ the Church is for all people

3. bishops   ___ the Church shares the holiness of Jesus

4. holy   ___ as the successors of the Apostles

I Will Do

I will remember that as a Catholic I have been called to help and serve other people as Jesus did.

This week, I will help

_____ by:
        (name)

_____

Remember

The Church worships and serves throughout the world.

The Church is one, holy, catholic, and apostolic.

The apostolic leaders of the Church are the pope and bishops.

Review

1. Describe what it means to belong to the Catholic Church.

2. Name the four marks of the Church.

3. How are the pope and bishops like St. Peter and the Apostles?

Family Note

This lesson describes what it means to belong to the Catholic Church today, which is one, holy, catholic, and apostolic. Encourage your child to carry out his or her decision to love and serve someone in particular this week.

Faith Words

sign:
something we see,
hear, touch or taste that
stands for something else.

sacrament:
a life-giving sign
given to the Church
by Jesus Christ.

Celebrating Together

We all enjoy celebrations. We often get together with our family and friends to celebrate important times in our lives.

Look at the chart on the next page. Talk about the things that we can see and hear at different celebrations. Tell about why each celebration is taking place.

You will notice an empty box in the Thanksgiving celebration. Write in something you might see on this day.

Choose one other time that your family celebrates, for example, Christmas. Write the name of the celebration on the chart. Talk about what you see and hear, and then tell why you celebrate.

Go over your chart with someone.

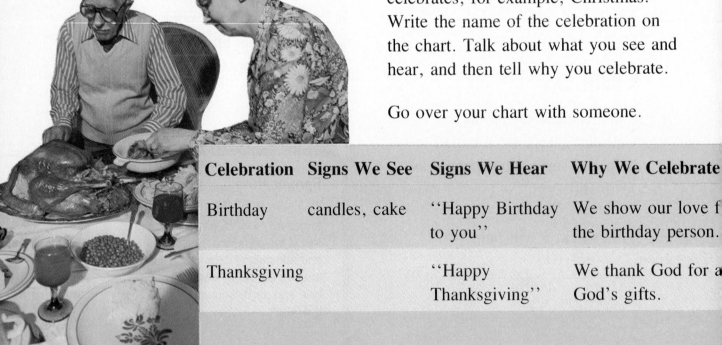

Celebration	Signs We See	Signs We Hear	Why We Celebrate
Birthday	candles, cake	"Happy Birthday to you"	We show our love f the birthday person.
Thanksgiving		"Happy Thanksgiving"	We thank God for a God's gifts.

The things we see, hear, touch, and taste at celebrations tell us why we celebrate. We call the things we see, hear, touch, and taste at celebrations *signs*.

Imagine what life would be like without celebrations. How would you feel?

We Will Learn

1 Jesus used signs to show His love.

2 The Catholic Church celebrates seven sacraments.

3 The sacraments are life-giving signs.

1 Jesus used signs to show His love.

Jesus often used life-giving signs to show people how deeply He loved them. Jesus touched sick people and healed them. He was kind to lonely people and made them happy. He forgave those who were sorry for their sins. He gave people new life.

By everything Jesus said and did, He showed us the power of God's love.

What signs did Jesus use to show people that He loved them?

Why were these signs called life-giving?

2 The Catholic Church celebrates seven sacraments.

In the Catholic Church, the sacraments are celebrations of our faith. They are signs of how Jesus is acting now in our lives. When we celebrate the sacraments, we are reminded that Jesus is still present and active among us. We meet Jesus in the sacraments and receive God's love and blessing.

We know that during His life on earth, Jesus gathered His friends together and formed them into His community, the Church. He wanted the Church to share God's own life with us through lasting signs that we could see and hear, taste and touch.

We call these signs the seven sacraments. Each of the sacraments tells us what God is doing in our lives. The chart on the next page will tell you more about the sacraments.

The Seven Sacraments

Sacraments We Celebrate	Signs We See	Signs We Hear	Why We Celebrate
Baptism	pouring of water	I baptize you. . . .	Jesus shares God's new life of grace with a person.
Confirmation	bishop anointing	Be sealed with the gift of the Holy Spirit.	Jesus sends the Holy Spirit to strengthen those confirmed.
Eucharist	bread and wine	This is My Body. This is My Blood.	Jesus shares His Body and Blood with us.
Reconciliation	priest makes the sign of the cross	I absolve you from your sins. . . .	Jesus forgives those who are sorry.
Anointing of the Sick	priest anoints sick person	Through this holy anointing . . . may the Lord save you and raise you up.	Jesus comforts and strengthens those who are sick.
Matrimony	joining of hands	I take you to be my wife (or husband) . . .	Jesus blesses the love of a man and a woman.
Holy Orders	bishop lays his hands on head of person being ordained.	Silence, followed by a special prayer for the person ordained.	Jesus sends us bishops, priests, and deacons to help us carry out the mission of Jesus.

Choose three of the above sacraments.
In your own words, describe each one.
Use the chart to help you.

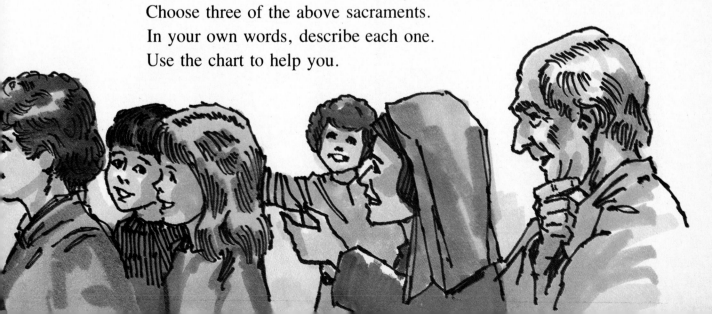

3 The sacraments are life-giving signs.

The sacraments are more than ordinary signs. Because Jesus is with us in the Church, the sacraments are truly life-giving signs. The sacraments give us a share in God's life and blessings. They show us how much God loves us. In each of the seven sacraments, we meet Jesus Christ, who shares God's own life of grace with us.

Each of the sacraments is a great prayer. In each of the sacraments, we praise and thank God for sharing God's life of grace with us. Each of the sacraments is also an invitation.

Do You Know

Here are the names of the seven sacraments that we celebrate in the Catholic Church.

The first three are known as the *sacraments of Initiation* or belonging. They are:
- Baptism
- Confirmation
- Eucharist

These two sacraments are known as the *sacraments of Healing*.
- Reconciliation
- Anointing of the Sick

These two sacraments are known as the *sacraments of Service*.
- Matrimony
- Holy Orders

42

We are invited to carry out the mission of Jesus in the world. We respond to the sacraments by the way we live our lives.

Talk about one of the sacraments that you have received.

Tell how receiving this sacrament has made a difference in your life.

I Have Learned

Do the puzzle.

S_____ are life-giving
          1A

_____ given to us by Jesus
     2D

_____ . God's life in us is
     3D

called _____ . Each
                    4D

sacrament has signs we can _____ ,
                               5A

_____ , touch or taste.
     6A

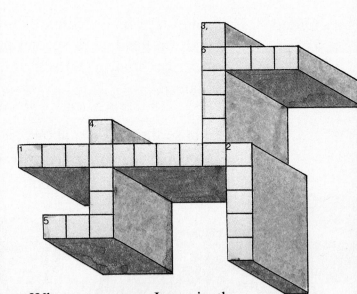

When you meet Jesus in the sacraments, what would you like your response to be?

I Will Do

Talk to a friend or family member about the signs of one of the sacraments. Use the chart on text page 41 to help you.

Prayer

Before we pray, we should stop, be quiet, and think about what we are going to do. Do that now before you pray.

God our Father, You give us new life through the signs of the sacraments, which tell us the wonders that You do for us. We ask You to help us to be faithful to the life You have given us. We ask this through Jesus Christ, Your Son, Our Lord. Amen.

Remember

The sacraments are life-giving signs. In each of the seven sacraments, we meet Jesus Christ, who shares God's own life of grace with us.

Review

1. What is a sacrament?

2. Name the seven sacraments.

3. Think about the next time you will receive Eucharist or Reconciliation. What can you do to prepare yourself better to receive these sacraments?

Family Note

In this lesson your child learned that sacraments are life-giving signs through which Jesus shares God's life of grace with us.

Help your child with this lesson by providing any pictures you have of family members celebrating the sacraments. Discuss your own feelings about the sacraments.

Unit II Test

Write the word from this word list that best fits each numbered definition. One is done for you.

sign   the sacraments
pope   baptized persons
Church   Ascension
Holy Spirit   bishops
followers of Jesus   a sacrament

1. A life-giving sign given to the Church by Jesus Christ

   _____

2. The successor of St. Peter as the leader of the whole Church

   _____

3. Something we see, hear, touch, or taste that stands for something else

   _____

4. The Third Person of the Blessed Trinity

   _____

5. Jesus' return to Heaven

   _____

6. The successors of the Apostles

   _____ bishops _____

7. The community of the baptized followers of Jesus Christ

   _____

8. Those who are united with Jesus and His Church

   _____

9. On Pentecost the Holy Spirit came to them.

   _____

10. They show us how much God loves us.

    _____

Answer briefly the questions on the lines provided.

11. What are the names of the sacraments of Initiation?

    _____

12. As a Catholic, what are you called on to do as Jesus did?

    _____

13. What are the names of the sacraments of Healing?

    _____

14. What is it the Holy Spirit helps the Church to do?

    _____

15. What are the names of the sacraments of Service?

    _____

From the list below, fill in the word, or words, that best completes the sentence.

holy	life-giving	signs	birthday
seven	Holy Spirit	understand	Pentecost
faith	one	life of grace	bishops
Good News	live up to	Helper	apostolic

16. Jesus told His followers to bring the _____ _____ of God's love to all the world.

17. After Jesus' Ascension, His followers waited for the coming of the _____ _____ .

18. Jesus had promised to send a _____ who would teach and help His followers forever.

19. The sacraments are _____ of how Jesus is acting now in our lives.

20. The _____ sacraments of our Catholic Church are _____ signs, celebrating our _____ .

21. We celebrate _____ as the _____ of the Church.

22. The Church is _____ , _____ , catholic and _____ .

23. In each of the sacraments, Jesus shares God's _____ _____ _____ with us.

24. What is the most important work of the Pope and the bishops?

_____

_____

25. How do your actions show that you are a follower of Jesus?

_____

_____

First Semester Test

Complete each sentence. Circle the letter of the correct ending.

1. The word *gospel* means
   a. "Follow Me."
   b. Good News.
   c. read the Bible daily.
   d. say your prayers every Sunday.

2. On the night before Jesus died,
   He promised to send a Helper.
   That Helper was
   a. Mary.
   b. the Pope.
   c. the Holy Spirit.
   d. the angel Gabriel.

3. In God's plan, human beings would
   a. never have to think.
   b. be forced to do God's will.
   c. become sick and die.
   d. be happy with God forever.

4. To say that the Church is
   apostolic means that
   a. our pope and bishops continue
      the work of Jesus and the Apostles.
   b. it is a small Church.
   c. its members are leaders.
   d. it is 3000 years old.

5. At the Annunciation God asked Mary to
   a. pray in the morning.
   b. become the Mother of God's
      Son Jesus.
   c. be silent.
   d. fear the angel.

6. At Pentecost the Spirit filled the
   disciples with
   a. laughter.
   b. fear.
   c. rules.
   d. the Holy Spirit.

7. When Jesus told His friends how
   to treat their enemies, He told
   them to
   a. hate their enemies.
   b. forgive them.
   c. ignore them.
   d. fight them.

8. The Sacraments of Initiation are
   Baptism, Confirmation and
   a. Anointing of the Sick.
   b. Holy Orders.
   c. Eucharist.
   d. Reconciliation.

9. The Sacraments of Healing are
   Reconciliation and
   a. Anointing of the Sick.
   b. Eucharist.
   c. Matrimony.
   d. Baptism.

10. Jesus left His followers to return
    to His Father in heaven on
    a. Easter morning.
    b. Pentecost.
    c. Good Friday.
    d. Ascension.

Complete the following quotations with words from the list. After each quotation write who said it.

with   follow   doing
happen   me   remember
am   Father   servant
forgive   Me   you
always   end

11. "Let it _____ to _____

as _____ have said."

_____

12. "_____ , _____ them,
they do not know what they are

_____ ." _____

13. "_____ , I will be _____ you

_____ until the _____ of time."

_____

14. "I _____ the Lord's _____ ."

_____

15. "Come, _____ _____ ."

_____

Complete each sentence. Circle the letter of the correct ending.

16. The Blessed Trinity is
   a. not hard to understand.
   b. three divine Persons in one God: God the Father, God the Son, and God the Holy Spirit.
   c. sacrament.
   d. a promise.

17. The sacraments are
   a. life-giving signs given to us by Jesus Christ.
   b. rules that we follow.
   c. dioceses of the Church.
   d. holy days.

18. The Bible is
   a. just for priests and lectors.
   b. a science book.
   c. the holy book of God's story.
   d. a gift of the Holy Spirit.

19. The Kingdom of God is
   a. a beautiful place in the sky.
   b. the power of love in the hearts and lives of people.
   c. a Corporal Work of Mercy.
   d. Peter and the Apostles.

20. Think first. Then answer this question. Are you happy to be a member of the Catholic Church? Tell why. (Use another piece of paper if you need to.)

_____

_____

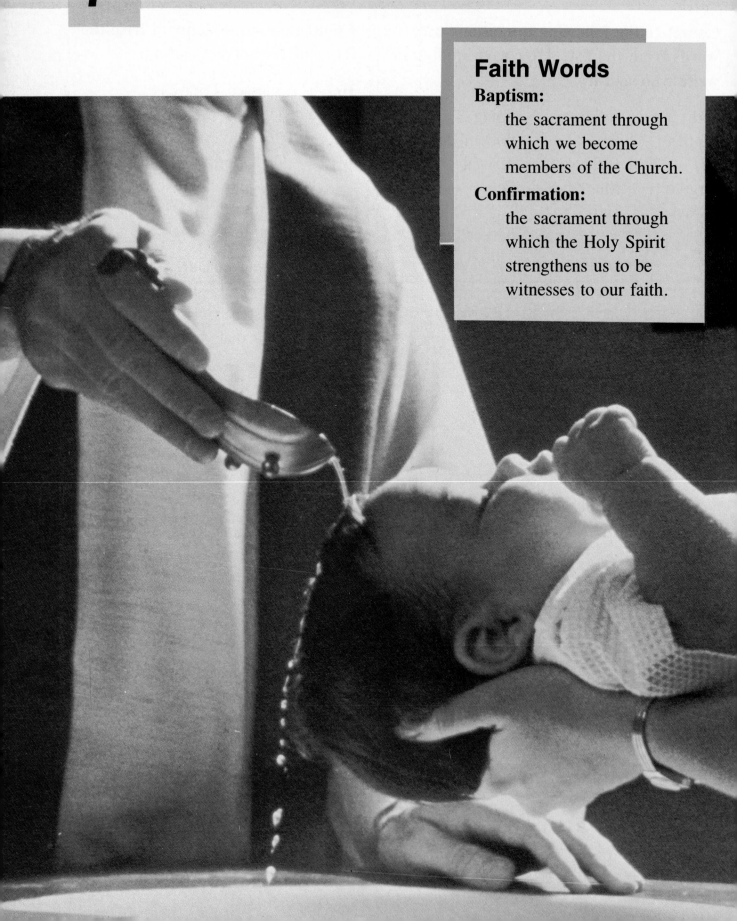

7 Becoming Catholic

Faith Words

Baptism:
the sacrament through which we become members of the Church.

Confirmation:
the sacrament through which the Holy Spirit strengthens us to be witnesses to our faith.

Welcome to the Church!

Tom and Ellen Matthews were as happy as they had been on their wedding day two years earlier. Once again they were surrounded by their family and friends in Holy Child Church. This time, all eyes were on their new baby, Michael. Soon the priest would enter the church, welcome everyone, and the celebration would begin.

"Just think, Tom," whispered Ellen, "in a few minutes, Michael will be baptized. This is a great day for all of us."

Tom looked down at the tiny face of the baby and then at all the smiling faces around them.

"OK, everybody," he said proudly. "Let's all welcome Michael to the Church."

Have you ever joined a new group?

How did you feel when you were welcomed?

Have you ever felt not welcome? Tell about it.

Why do you think welcoming is such an important part of Baptism?

We Will Learn

1 In the sacrament of Baptism, we are welcomed into the Church.

2 Baptism frees us from sin and gives us God's life.

3 Confirmation makes us witnesses to our faith.

1 In the sacrament of Baptism, we are welcomed into the Church.

Jesus taught His followers that He welcomed everyone. One day some people brought children to Jesus for His blessing. The followers of Jesus tried to keep the children away, but Jesus welcomed them instead. He took the children in His arms, placed His hands on each of them, and blessed them (Mark 10:13–16).

The Church has always welcomed everyone who wishes to belong. The Church does this through the three sacraments of Initiation: Baptism, Eucharist, and Confirmation.

At Baptism, the priest or deacon welcomes us in the name of the whole Christian community. In this way, the sacrament begins. We welcome each new member with great joy into the Christian family, the Church.

In Baptism, each of us receives a Christian name. This is a sign of our belonging to the Church.

During the ceremony, the priest or deacon pours water over the head of the person being baptized, saying, "*(name)*, I baptize you in the name of the Father, and of the Son, and of the Holy Spirit."

Through Baptism we receive the Holy Spirit. We are made children of God and brothers and sisters of Jesus. Because most of us are baptized as babies, our parents and godparents promise to help us grow up as good Christians.

What does it mean to be baptized into the Catholic Church?

Why are godparents so important in the life of a young Catholic?

Do You Know

We are baptized in the name of the three Persons in God, the Blessed Trinity—God the Father, God the Son, and God the Holy Spirit. The Trinity is the basic truth of our Christian faith. It means that we believe that there are three Persons in one God.

2 Baptism frees us from sin and gives us God's life.

From the Bible, we learn that the first people sinned and rejected God's special life of grace within them. This sin is called *original sin*. All of us have been born into this world with original sin.

Baptism frees us from original sin and gives us a share in God's own life which we call *grace*. We are God's own children. The Bible tells us, "See how much the Father has loved us! The Father's love is so great that we are called God's children—and so, in fact, we are" (1 John 3:1).

What does Baptism do for us?

Today, how can you show others that you are a baptized Catholic?

3 Confirmation makes us witnesses to our faith.

The sacrament of Confirmation is another step in our initiation into the Church. When we are confirmed, God the Holy Spirit comes to us as our Helper and Guide. In this sacrament, the person being confirmed is sealed or anointed with holy oil. The bishop says to him or her: "Be sealed with the Gift of the Holy Spirit." The confirmed Catholic goes forth to share his or her faith with all people.

When we are confirmed, the Holy Spirit strengthens us with special gifts that help us live as faithful followers and witnesses to Jesus Christ. These gifts are: wisdom and understanding, right judgment and courage, knowledge and reverence, wonder and awe in God's presence. You might want to look these words up in your *Glossary*.

Baptism and Confirmation are two sacraments of Initiation, or belonging. Through these sacraments we celebrate our membership in the Church. In the next lesson we will learn about the third sacrament of Initiation, the Eucharist.

What does the Holy Spirit do for us in Confirmation?

What can confirmed Catholics do to show they are followers of Jesus?

I Have Learned

Circle the correct answer.

In Baptism, the Holy Spirit fills the one being baptized with
- water.
- grace.
- holy oil.

Baptism frees us from
- God's life.
- our parents.
- original sin.

Confirmation makes us
- witnesses to our faith.
- forget about others.
- share our faith only with our family.

In Baptism we are welcomed into
- a club.
- the Church.
- our family.

Why must you learn as much as you can about being a Catholic?

What do you like most about being a Catholic?

52

I Will Do

Find out all you can about your own Baptism. Does your family have any pictures to recall that special day?

Who are your godparents? Write their names here.

_____

_____

Prayer

Each sacrament is a great prayer. When we celebrate the sacraments, we are praying with the whole Church. Let us thank God for the sacraments.

Father, we thank You for all the sacraments, which are signs of Your unseen power.

Help us to keep alive the light of faith in us. Make us true witnesses to You and to Your love for us. We ask this through Jesus Christ our Lord. Amen.

Remember

In Baptism we are:
- freed from original sin;
- given God's new life;
- welcomed into the Church.

Confirmation makes us witnesses to our faith.

Review

1. What happens in the sacrament of Baptism?

2. What does the Holy Spirit strengthen us to do in Confirmation?

3. What can you do to share your faith with others?

Family Note

In this lesson, your child has learned about the sacraments of Baptism and Confirmation. Encourage him or her to spend time talking with you about what it means to be baptized and confirmed.

8 The Sacrament of the Eucharist

Faith Words

Eucharist:
the sacrament of the Body and Blood of Jesus Christ.

Holy Communion:
the receiving of the Body and Blood of Jesus Christ.

The Best Gift

How exciting it is to find a gift with your name on it. Everyone loves to open a gift and find out what is inside.

When we love people we want to choose the best gifts for them. We look for things that will make them happy.

There are some gifts that cannot be put in a box. We cannot put a smile in a box, but a smile is a wonderful gift. We cannot tie a bow on a hug, but a hug is a wonderful gift.

The best gift we can give others is ourselves! When we love others, we give them our love and our time. We listen to their stories. We cry with them when they are sad. We laugh with them when they are happy.

Do you like to receive gifts?

What is the best gift you have ever received? Why?

Have you ever thought of yourself as a gift? In what way?

How can you be a gift to another person?

54

We Will Learn

1 Jesus gave us Himself in the Eucharist.

2 We celebrate the Eucharist at Mass.

3 We are united to Christ in the Eucharist.

1 Jesus gave us Himself in the Eucharist.

Jesus showed how much He loves us by giving us the wonderful gift of Himself in the Eucharist. At the Last Supper on the night before He died, Jesus celebrated the feast of Passover with His friends. During the meal, Jesus took bread and gave thanks to God. He gave the bread to His friends and said, "Take this, all of you, and eat it; this is My Body which will be given up for you" (from Luke 22:19).

Then He took a cup of wine and gave thanks to God. He gave the cup to His friends and said, "Take this, all of you, and drink from it; this is the cup of My Blood" (from Luke 22:20).

The bread and wine were now the Body and Blood of Jesus Christ, even though they still looked and tasted like bread and wine. Jesus told His friends, "Do this in memory of me" (Luke 22:19).

Ever since that Last Supper, the community of Jesus, the Church, has continued to "do this in memory" of Jesus. At Mass we offer bread or wine to God. Through the words and actions of the priest and the power of the Holy Spirit, the bread and wine become the Body and Blood of Jesus. We call this the Eucharist.

Jesus continues to give Himself to us in the Eucharist. We receive the Body and Blood of Jesus Christ in *Holy Communion*.

What gift did Jesus give us at the Last Supper?

Why do we continue to celebrate the Eucharist?

56

2 We celebrate the Eucharist at Mass.

After the death and resurrection of Jesus, His friends often came together to pray and to remember what Jesus had told them. They shared the Body and Blood of Jesus under the appearance of bread and wine. They were happy that Jesus still remained with them in the Eucharist.

Today, the friends of Jesus still celebrate the Eucharist together. The priest says the words that

Jesus said at the Last Supper over the bread and wine. The bread and wine become Jesus' Body and Blood. We share the Body and Blood of Jesus in Holy Communion. Jesus gives us the gift of Himself to nourish us and to help us live as members of His Church.

The celebration of the Eucharist is called the *Mass*. The Mass is our great prayer of praise and thanks to God. That is why the Church requires that all Catholics join with others to take part in the Mass every Saturday evening or Sunday.

When we take part in our parish celebration of the Eucharist, we show that we appreciate the great gift Jesus has given us— the gift of Himself.

What did Jesus ask His friends to do during the Last Supper?

Why should we take part in the Mass every Saturday or Sunday and as often as we can during the week?

The Last Supper, Ugolino Da Nerio. Early 14th Century.

Do You Know

As a sign of respect and to remind us of the spiritual nourishment we are about to receive, the Church asks us not to take any food or drink (except water) for one hour before receiving Holy Communion.

3 We are united to Christ in the Eucharist

In the Eucharist, Jesus makes us one with Him and with one another. He invites us to share with Him His meal and His sacrifice.

The Eucharist is a *meal* because in Holy Communion we share the Body and Blood of Christ as our food.

The Eucharist is also a *sacrifice*. Jesus sacrificed and gave up His life for us on the cross. Each time we celebrate the Eucharist we remember that Jesus gave up His life for us. In the Eucharist we share in His sacrifice.

Each time we receive Jesus in Holy Communion we receive the Body and Blood of Jesus Christ. We are united to Him and to one another.

Receiving Jesus gives us the opportunity to ask Him to help us live as He wishes us to live.

How is the Eucharist a meal? a sacrifice?

Why is it important for us to share the Body and Blood of Christ?

58

I Have Learned

Fill in the chart below with the words of Jesus at the Last Supper.

"This is _____ _____."

"This is _____ _____."

"Do _____ __ _____ __ ___."

What can you do to thank Jesus for giving us Himself in the Eucharist?

I Will Do

When is the next time that you will go to Mass? Decide now what you will do to better prepare to take part in the Eucharist.

Prayer

Prayers do not have to be long to be prayers. Here is a short prayer from the Bible.

Come, Lord Jesus!

Remember

The Eucharist is the sacrament of the Body and Blood of Jesus Christ.

When we celebrate the Eucharist at Mass, we are united to Christ and to one another.

The Eucharist is a meal and a sacrifice.

Review

1. What is the Eucharist?

2. Why do we celebrate the Eucharist?

3. How is the Eucharist a meal and a sacrifice?

4. How can you thank God for the gift of Jesus in the Eucharist?

Family Note

This lesson focused on the Eucharist as the Body and Blood of Jesus, who gave us the gift of Himself in the Last Supper.

You might want to tell or read aloud from the Bible the story of the Lord's Supper (Luke 22:14-20).

9 The Mass

Faith Words

liturgy:
the way we worship God in the Catholic Church.

Mass:
the celebration of the Eucharist.

Taking Part

Joan was bored. She was restless, and her mind kept wandering. This often happened when she was at Mass.

Her little brother Matt did not help much. He had to be picked up often, or he would climb all over, kick the kneeler, and make it impossible to hear what was being said.

Joan wished she were home, listening to music, laughing, playing with friends—anything. But her mom and dad said she had to come to Mass and "take part."

What, Joan asked herself, did that mean? Nan McGill and her family got to bring up the gifts one week, but no one ever asked her family to do that.

Joan felt her mom's hand touch her shoulder. Joan stopped fidgeting and met her mom's eyes. "Sing," said her mother. Then she sang "Be . . . not . . . afraid. . . ." She nodded for Joan to join in.

Her mom smiled as Joan started to sing. Joan liked to sing and felt more a part of the celebration. Her mom smiled her encouragement. "That's right," she whispered. "Take part."

What is your favorite way to take part at Mass?

Have you ever been bored at Mass?

What do you do about it?

Can you remember enjoying a celebration of the Mass? Tell about it.

We Will Learn

1 At Mass we listen to God's Word from the Bible.

2 At Mass we offer and receive the gift of Jesus.

3 We bring God's love to others.

1 At Mass we listen to God's Word from the Bible.

The Mass is our celebration of the Eucharist. At the beginning of Mass, God's people come together. We make the Sign of the Cross with the priest, who greets us in Jesus' name. Together, we recall our sins and ask for God's mercy. We prepare to listen to God's Word by asking for forgiveness for our sins.

Then we begin the part of the Mass called the *Liturgy of the Word*. During this part of the Mass, we listen to readings from the Bible, God's Holy Word. God speaks to us through these readings. We hear what God has done for us and how God wants us to live.

After the readings, the priest or deacon explains their meaning for our lives. Together, we say the Creed, which says that we believe in all that the Church teaches. Then we pray together for the needs of our Church and all God's people.

How does God speak to us in the Liturgy of the Word?

For whom or for what would you like to pray the next time you go to Mass?

2 At Mass we offer and receive the gift of Jesus.

In the Mass we offer gifts to God. We begin the *Liturgy of the Eucharist* by presenting our gifts of bread and wine to the priest. These gifts are a sign that we give to God all that we are and do. The priest accepts our gifts and prepares the bread and wine. Our gifts of bread and wine will become for us the Body and Blood of Jesus Christ.

Then the priest begins the part of the Mass called the *Eucharistic Prayer*. He says and does what Jesus did at the Last Supper. He says over the bread and wine, "This is My body. . . . This is My blood. . . ." The bread and wine become the Body and Blood of Jesus Christ. This is called the *consecration*. Then in the name of all those present, the priest gives thanks to God by offering up the Body and Blood of Jesus. All present sing or say Amen as the Eucharistic prayer ends.

At this time in the Mass we pray the Lord's Prayer together and give one another a sign of God's peace. At Communion time, we share the holy meal of the Eucharist. We go to the altar and receive Jesus Himself in Holy Communion, either in our hands or on our tongues.

What gifts do we offer to God at Mass?

What gift does God give us in return?

3 We bring God's love to others.

At the end of Mass, the priest blesses us and says, "Go in peace to love and serve the Lord."

We try to do this each day by bringing the peace and love of Jesus to everyone we meet. We try to share our time and talents with them. We try to care for the poor, the sick, and the lonely people around us. We try to bring God's peace and love to everyone we meet.

The next time you go to Mass, how will you take part?

How can you live the Mass in your family? among your friends?

I Have Learned

Fill in the blanks. Choose the correct answer from among the words listed.

1. At the beginning of Mass, God's people

   _____ .

   a. begin the rosary
   b. come together
   c. bring up the gifts

2. God _____ to us in the Liturgy of the Word.
   a. sings
   b. speaks
   c. prays

3. In the Liturgy of the _____ , the bread and wine become the Body and Blood of Jesus Christ.
   a. Bible
   b. Word
   c. Eucharist

I Will Do

When you go to Mass this week, listen carefully to the readings from the Bible.
What one lesson did you learn?

Choose one way you can live this lesson in your everyday life.

Prayer

The friends of Jesus once came to Him and asked Him to teach them to pray. This is the prayer Jesus taught them.

Our Father, who art in heaven,
hallowed be Thy name;
Thy kingdom come;
Thy will be done on earth
as it is in heaven.
Give us this day our daily bread;
and forgive us our trespasses
as we forgive those
who trespass against us;
and lead us not into temptation,
but deliver us from evil. Amen.

Remember

At Mass, we listen to God's Word from the Bible. We offer our gifts of bread and wine and receive the Body and Blood of Christ in Holy Communion. We go from Mass to bring God's love to others.

Review

1. What happens during the Liturgy of the Word?

2. What happens during the Liturgy of the Eucharist?

3. How does God speak to you at Mass? How can you show God your love at Mass?

Family Note

In this lesson your child learned about the different parts of the Mass. You may want to read this Sunday's Gospel with your child and talk about what it means to you.

Unit III Test

Write the word from this list that best fits each numbered definition. One is done for you.

Liturgy　　　　Holy Spirit
Holy Communion　Eucharist
The Trinity　　　Confirmation
Eucharistic Prayer　The Mass
Baptism　　　　Liturgy of the Word

1. "Be sealed with the Gift of the Holy Spirit."

   _____

2. Through this, we are made children of God and brothers and sisters of Jesus.

   _____

3. Our great prayer of praise and thanks to God.

   _____

4. Fills with grace the person being baptized.

   _____

5. We hear readings from the Bible, God's Holy Word.

   _____

6. The basic truth of our Christian faith.

   _____The Trinity_____

7. Each time we celebrate this sacrament, we remember and share in Jesus' sacrifice.

   _____

8. Receiving the Body and Blood of Jesus Christ.

   _____

9. The way we worship in the Catholic Church.

   _____

10. During this prayer, the priest says and does what Jesus did at the Last Supper.

    _____

Answer these questions.

11. What is the name of the celebration of the Eucharist?

_____

12. What sacrament makes us witnesses to our faith?

_____

13. In the Eucharist, what is the gift Jesus gives us?

_____

14. When we leave at the end of Mass, what is it we try to bring to others?

_____

15. In Baptism what are we freed from?

_____

16. When we are confirmed, who comes to us as our Helper and Guide?

_____

17. What is the sacrament that welcomes us into the Church?

_____

18. What is the Sign we make at the beginning of the Mass?

_____

19. What happens at each celebration of the Eucharist?

_____

_____

20. Why do you think the Mass is the greatest prayer of all?

_____

_____

Faith Words

Ten Commandments:
the basic laws of God.

Law of Love:
love of God and
neighbor.

Good Rules

The late winter day was already dark when Peter finished basketball practice and started home. He liked his new school and the new friends he was beginning to make. Peter was so wrapped up in his thoughts that he did not hear the toot of the horn behind him and didn't notice the car until it pulled up beside him.

"Would you like a ride?" the man asked.

Peter looked at him, his heart pumping. All the safety warnings he had heard at home and from the visiting police officer at school went running through his mind. He was about to take off down the street when the light went on inside the car. The man repeated, "Peter, can we give you a lift home?"

Peter saw his new friend Mike Lanson waving to him from the passenger seat.

Peter grinned. "Thanks, Mr. Lanson," he said as he climbed into the back seat. "Good for you, Peter," said Mr. Lanson. "You were wise to make sure who we were before getting into the car."

What safety rules do you think Peter had heard at home and at school?

Why do you think people make rules for our safety?

What makes a rule a good rule?

We Will Learn

1 The Ten Commandments tell us how to live as God's people.

2 The first three commandments tell us how to love God.

3 The other commandments tell us how to love others and ourselves.

1 The Ten Commandments tell us how to live as God's people.

Long ago God gave the people of Israel Ten Commandments or laws for their safety and freedom. This is the story of the Ten Commandments.

The Bible tells us that in very early times the people of Israel lived as slaves in Egypt. But God had chosen the Israelites to be God's own people—the ones who would know and worship only the one true God. This was hard for them because they were slaves of the Egyptians who worshiped many false gods. To help them God gave them a great leader called Moses.

Moses helped the Israelites escape from Egypt. He led them to safety and freedom in the desert.

In return God asked them to join in a solemn agreement, or *covenant*. God said, "If you will obey me and keep my covenant, you will be my own people, my chosen people" (Exodus 19:5). The people promised to obey God and keep the covenant. Then God gave Moses the laws of the covenant called the *Ten Commandments*. The Ten Commandments would help God's people remain faithful to the one, true God and to be truly safe and free.

The chart on the next page lists the Ten Commandments and tells what each one means.

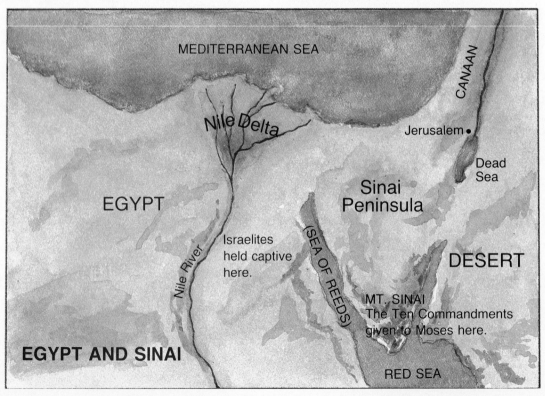

EGYPT AND SINAI

MEDITERRANEAN SEA

CANAAN

Nile Delta

Jerusalem •

Dead Sea

EGYPT

Sinai Peninsula

Israelites held captive here.

(SEA OF REEDS)

Nile River

DESERT

MT. SINAI
The Ten Commandments given to Moses here.

RED SEA

The Ten Commandments	What the Commandments Mean for Us
1. I am the Lord your God, who brought you out of slavery. Worship no gods except Me.	God must come first in our lives. No one or no thing can be more important to us than God.
2. You shall not misuse the name of the Lord your God.	We must respect the names of God, Jesus, holy places, and Holy Days.
3. Remember to keep holy the Sabbath day.	We should rest from work and worship God together on Sundays and Holy Days.
4. Honor your father and your mother.	We must love, honor, and obey our parents or guardians.
5. You shall not kill.	We should respect and care for the gift of life and live peacefully.
6. You shall not commit adultery.	Husbands and wives should be faithful to one another.
7. You shall not steal.	We should not take or destroy what belongs to others.
8. You shall not tell lies against your neighbor.	We should respect the truth.
9. You shall not want your neighbor's wife or husband.	We should protect the holiness of marriage.
10. You shall not want to take your neighbor's possessions.	We should respect the rights and property of others.

From Exodus 20:2-17

Name the Ten Commandments. Choose one commandment and explain what it means to you.

Do You Know

One day a man asked Jesus which of God's laws was the most important. Jesus answered, ''Love the Lord your God with all your heart, with all your soul, with all your mind. . . . Love your neighbor as you love yourself'' (Matthew 22:37–39). We call this greatest law of all the *Law of Love*.

2 The first three commandments tell us how to love God.

The First Commandment means that God must come before everyone and everything else in our lives. The Second Commandment reminds us that God's name is holy and must be used with love and respect.

The Third Commandment tells us to "keep holy the Sabbath day." The word *Sabbath* means "rest." For Catholics, Sunday is the Sabbath day. Going to Mass each Sunday is the best way to keep the Sabbath day holy.

How do the first three commandments help you to love God better?

3 The other commandments tell us how to love others and ourselves.

The Fourth Commandment tells us to honor our parents. Because our parents have given us life, we owe them love, respect, and care. We should also show respect for our guardians, our teachers, and older members of our families.

The Fifth Commandment reminds us that all life is a gift of God. We must not do anything that would harm others, our bodies, or our minds. The Sixth and Ninth Commandments tell us to treat with respect our bodies and those of others. The Seventh and Tenth Commandments forbid stealing or destroying what belongs to others.

The Eighth Commandment requires us to tell the truth. It forbids lying and the kind of gossip that hurts others.

Today, the Ten Commandments show us how to remain faithful to God. They help us to live together in peace and love. God has given us these laws for our safety and freedom.

How do these commandments help us to love God and our neighbor better?

72

I Have Learned

Choose three commandments. Tell how they help us live as God's people.

I Will Do

The Commandments are not just laws that tell us what we *must not do*. The Commandments also tell us what we *must do* to be God's people. Choose one of the commandments. Tell what you will do today or tomorrow to keep that commandment.

Example: Today I will keep the Fourth Commandment by finding one way to make my family's life happier or easier.

Prayer

At times we pray to thank God for God's great gifts to us. Use this prayer to thank God for the laws that help us live in safety and freedom.

God, You have given us Your
    laws
and told us to obey them
    faithfully.
How I hope that I shall be
    faithful
    in keeping Your laws!

From Psalm 119:4–5

Remember

The Ten Commandments are the laws God gave us to help us live as God's people.

The Commandments help us to love God above all things and our neighbor as ourselves.

Review

1. Name the Ten Commandments.

2. Which commandments require us to love God? Which commandments require us to love our neighbor?

3. How did Jesus answer the question, "What is the most important commandment?"

4. How will you practice this commandment this week?

Family Note

This lesson focuses on the Ten Commandments. Help your child to see that God's laws are meant to free us to live with one another in peace and harmony.

11 The Beatitudes

Faith Words

Beatitudes:
Jesus' guidelines for true happiness.

The First Camping Trip

"Tomorrow's the day!" Janet shouted to her friend Rosa as they walked home after school.

"Yep! My sleeping bag is packed, and I'm ready to go," replied Rosa.

The two girls were new members of the Junior Wilderness Club. Saturday morning they were leaving with the Club on their first overnight camping trip. They had been looking forward to it for months.

Later that evening, the phone rang at Janet's. It was Rosa. "I can't go," she whispered.

"What do you mean?" Janet asked.

Rosa told Janet that her mother had gone to the hospital and that she had to stay at home with her grandfather who could not be left alone. "I hope you'll have a good time. Goodbye, Janet," Rosa said as she hung up the phone.

74

Rosa was so happy she could hardly believe her ears. All weekend the two girls camped at Rosa's house. They helped Rosa's grandfather. And they had fun.

Janet went home feeling great. She said to her mother, "I think happiness is helping someone, isn't it, Mom?" Janet's mother hugged her daughter.

What had Janet expected to do? Do you think she was disappointed?

What surprising results did her decision bring?

Have you ever made a decision that:
- you thought would make you happy but did not?
- you thought would spoil your happiness but instead made it even greater?

The next morning Janet was up early. She told her mother what she wanted to do. She put her sleeping bag on her shoulder and left the apartment. She went straight to Rosa's house. When Rosa opened the door, Janet said, "I'm not going without you! Let's have our camping trip right here. OK? And we can cook our hot dogs for your grandfather! OK?"

We Will Learn

1 Jesus teaches the people about true happiness.

2 The Beatitudes are guidelines for true happiness.

3 We try to live with faith, hope, and love.

75

1 Jesus teaches the people about true happiness.

One day when some very large crowds were following Jesus, He went up the side of a hill to speak to them about what it means to be really happy. Jesus told the people not to worry about things, about what they would wear or what they would eat. Then He told them how the wildflowers and the birds live. "Look at the birds of the air," He said, "They do not plant seeds yet your Father in heaven takes care of them. And look at how the wild flowers grow. They do not make clothes for themselves, but no king ever had clothes as beautiful as these!" Then Jesus told the people, "If God cares for these little things, how much more God cares for you! Be concerned above everything else with the Kingdom of God and God will take care of all the rest" (from Matthew 6:25–33).

The people listened and thought about the lesson of happiness— how we live will bring us more happiness than what we eat or wear.

What did Jesus teach us about worrying about things like what to wear or what to eat?

2 The Beatitudes are guide— lines for true happiness.

Jesus gave the people some guidelines for true happiness. We call these guidelines the *Beatitudes*. Beatitude is a word that means "way to happiness." The beginning word of each Beatitude is *Happy*—a good clue to what the Beatitudes are all about. Look at the chart on the next page. It names the Beatitudes and tells you something about what each one means.

The Beautitudes	What the Beautitudes Mean for Us
"Happy are the poor in Spirit: The Kingdom of God is theirs."	People who are *poor in spirit* know that they need God's help and ask for it.
"Happy are those who are gentle: They will receive what God has promised."	People who are *gentle* are kind. They are patient with others.
"Happy are those who mourn: They shall be comforted."	People who *mourn* are sad at the sin and suffering around them. They remember that God is our Great Comforter.
"Happy are those who hunger and thirst for justice: They shall be satisfied."	People who are *just* share what they have with others. They try to be fair to everyone.
"Happy are those who show mercy: God will be merciful with them."	People who are *merciful* are always willing to forgive.
"Happy are the pure of heart: They shall see God."	People who are *pure of heart* always put God first in their lives.
"Happy are the peacemakers: They are God's own children."	People who are *peacemakers* bring peace and reconciliation to everyone, everywhere.
"Happy are those who are persecuted for doing God's will: The Kingdom *of God* is theirs."	People of *great courage* are willing to suffer to do what they know is right.
From Matthew 5:1-11	What are the Beatitudes?
	Choose one Beatitude, and explain what it means to you.

3 We try to live with faith, hope, and love.

The Beatitudes are wonderful guidelines for living as followers of Jesus. They are also very surprising because they turn our ideas about happiness upside down. They are not quite what we had in mind about being happy! But if we want to be followers of Jesus, we will try to live according to the Beatitudes. To help us do this, God gives us the gifts of faith, hope, and love.

- We live as people of *faith* by believing in God's Word even when the world around us seems to be full of sin and suffering.

- We live as people of *hope* by trusting in Jesus and His promises of the Kingdom and eternal life.

- We live as people of *love* by freely loving and serving others as Jesus showed us how to do: "Love one another. As I have loved you, so you must love one another" (John 13:34).

When we live with faith, hope, and love, we gradually come to understand and live the happiness that Jesus was teaching us about in the Beatitudes.

Name one way you can be a person of faith, of hope, of love.

I Have Learned

Read the Beatitude chart. Choose one of the Beatitudes, and tell what it means to you.

I Will Do

Think of someone you know or have read about who lives according to the Beatitudes. Tell someone why you chose that person.

What does it mean to be a Beatitude person?

What can you do to be more of a Beatitude person today?

Will you do it?

Prayer

This prayer can help us to live as Beatitude people.

Lord, make me an instrument
    of Your peace.
Where there is hatred, let me
    sow love.
Where there is injury, pardon.
Where there is despair, hope.
Where there is sadness, joy.

Remember

Jesus taught us the Beatitudes as guidelines for being truly happy. We try to live the Beatitudes with faith, hope, and love.

Review

1. Name three of the Beatitudes.

2. Choose one Beatitude. Tell how you can live this Beatitude in your home.

3. Read the last Beatitude. Name a time when you will need courage to do what God wants you to do.

Family Note

This lesson emphasized the Beatitudes and the virtues of faith, hope, and love. Help your child to see that these guidelines enable us to live in peace and harmony with one another.

Faith Words

absolution:
a sign of God's forgiveness.

sin:
freely choosing to do something which we know is wrong and against God's will.

conscience:
the ability to know right from wrong.

Laurie's Choice

"Some kids say it's cool to get away with shoplifting at the Mall. They say if you won't even try, you're chicken."

Laurie was talking to her friend Carla on the way home from school. She wondered if she was missing out on something by never attempting to steal anything in a crowded department store.

"That's not for me," Carla answered. "I know better. Stealing is wrong— whether you get caught or not. It is taking what is not yours."

Laurie still was not sure. She thought about all the popular kids who said they had taken cassettes or jewelry "just for the fun of it." She wondered if she should try stealing, too.

If you were Laurie's friend, what would you say to her about shoplifting?

Why do you think some people feel it is okay to steal in a large store?

We Will Learn

1. Sin is freely choosing to do what we know is wrong.

2. We examine our conscience before Reconciliation.

3. Reconciliation is a sacrament of God's mercy.

81

1 Sin is freely choosing to do what we know is wrong.

Everyday we have to make choices or decisions as Laurie did. Sometimes, like Laurie, we feel like doing something wrong. This is called a *temptation*. A temptation is not a sin unless we give in to it and do what is wrong. *Sin* is freely choosing to do what we know is wrong and against God's will. We sin when:

- we know that something is wrong and it is against God's law;
- we think about doing it;
- we freely decide to do it.

Some sins are very serious. They destroy our friendship with God. The Church calls these mortal sins. *Mortal sins* separate us from God. Some sins called venial sins are less serious. *Venial sins* weaken our friendship with God.

We are responsible for our sins and the damage and hurt they cause. We are also responsible for not doing the good things we should do.

What is the difference between a temptation and a sin?

2 We examine our conscience before Reconciliation.

Our conscience helps us to make decisions about what is right and wrong. *Conscience* is the ability to know what is right or wrong, what we should or should not do.

Learning how to make decisions about right and wrong is called *forming our conscience*. We learn to form our conscience by following:

- the teaching of the Church;
- the advice of our parents;
- and the guidance of the Holy Spirit.

It is important to learn how to *examine* our *conscience*. This means we think about our thoughts and actions. We ask ourselves if we have loved God, others, and ourselves.

3 Reconciliation is a sacrament of God's mercy.

To *reconcile* means to make friends with someone again. When we sin, we need to be reconciled with God. That is just what happens in the sacrament of Reconciliation. We reestablish the friendship between us and God and the entire Christian community. We celebrate God's love and forgiveness and our forgiveness of one another.

Before we celebrate the sacrament of Reconciliation, we take time to examine our conscience. We do not have to remember every little fault. We should focus on a main weakness that separates us from God's life of grace and causes us to sin. We should discuss this with the priest.

After the priest listens to us tell, or confess, our sins, he talks with us about how we can be better. He then gives us a *penance* which is a good deed to do or prayers to say. Doing the penance is our way of showing that we are really sorry for what we have done wrong. We pray an Act of Contrition. The priest then gives *absolution*, or forgiveness. The words and actions of the priest are signs that God has forgiven us.

An Examination of Conscience

In examining our conscience, we ask ourselves questions like these based on the Ten Commandments and the Law of Love.

- Have I gone to Mass every week on Saturday night or Sunday?

- Have I used God's name with reverence and respect?

- Have I obeyed my parents or guardians?

- Have I taken something that belongs to someone else?

- Have I done things that are harmful to my body? or to the body of someone else?

- Have I been truthful and fair?

83

We should always examine our conscience before celebrating the sacrament of Reconciliation.

What helps us to form our conscience?

What questions would you add to the Examination of Conscience?

There are two ordinary ways of celebrating the sacrament of Reconciliation—the *Individual Rite* and the *Communal Rite*. Both ways of celebrating Reconciliation with the priest are outlined on the inside back cover of this book.

Look at the Individual Rite of Reconciliation. What happens during this celebration?

Look at the Communal (with others) Rite. What happens during this celebration?

Whether we celebrate the sacrament of Reconciliation alone or with others, we confess our sins to the priest and receive absolution by ourselves. This sacrament is a wonderful way to praise and thank God for the gifts of mercy and forgiveness. It is a way to grow in God's life of grace and in love of one another.

Have you ever been reconciled with another person? How?

Why do we call the sign of God's love and forgiveness the sacrament of Reconciliation?

I Have Learned

Number these events in the order in which they happen during the sacrament of Reconciliation. Number them 1 to 5.

_____ The priest absolves us from our sins.

_____ We tell our sins to the priest.

_____ We say an Act of Contrition.

_____ The priest gives us a penance.

_____ The priest talks with us about how to do better.

I Will Do

Spend a few minutes of quiet time in a place where you can be alone. Ask God the Holy Spirit for the wisdom to know yourself and to see where you need to improve in your love for God and for others. Just sit quietly, and give God a chance to guide you. Try to do this once a week. Act according to what you learn from the Holy Spirit within you.

Prayer

At times, and especially in the sacrament of Reconciliation, we tell God we are sorry for our sins. Here is a prayer of sorrow, or contrition, that you can pray.

O my God,
I am sorry for my sins.
In choosing to sin,
and failing to do good,
I have sinned against You
and Your Church.
I firmly intend,
with the help of Your Son,
to make up for my sins
and to love as I should.

Remember

In the sacrament of Reconciliation, we show we are sorry for our sins and receive God's forgiveness through the words and actions of the priest.

Review

1. What is sin?

2. What is mortal sin?

3. What is venial sin?

4. What do we celebrate in the sacrament of Reconciliation?

5. If you have hurt someone or done something wrong, what will you do to show you are sorry?

Family Note

This lesson focused on the sacrament of Reconciliation (Penance) and the nature of sin. It emphasized that God will always forgive our sins if we are sorry. Share your feelings about how you have experienced God's forgiveness in your life.

Faith Words

Corporal Works of Mercy:
    ways we can help those who suffer physically.

Spiritual Works of Mercy:
    ways we can help those who suffer in mind, heart or spirit.

When Did We See You . . .?

Do you ever see poor people on the street?

How do you feel when you see on TV pictures of children going hungry?

What do you think of when you see someone who is homeless?

Imagine someone who is hungry, thirsty, or homeless. Try to see yourself and your family helping that person. What would you do?

Sometimes when we see people in need, we feel helpless. "That's terrible," we tell ourselves. But then we ask, "What can I do about it?"

We Will Learn

1 Jesus tells us about the Last Judgment.

2 Jesus asks us to care for the physical needs of others.

3 Jesus asks us to care for the spiritual needs of others.

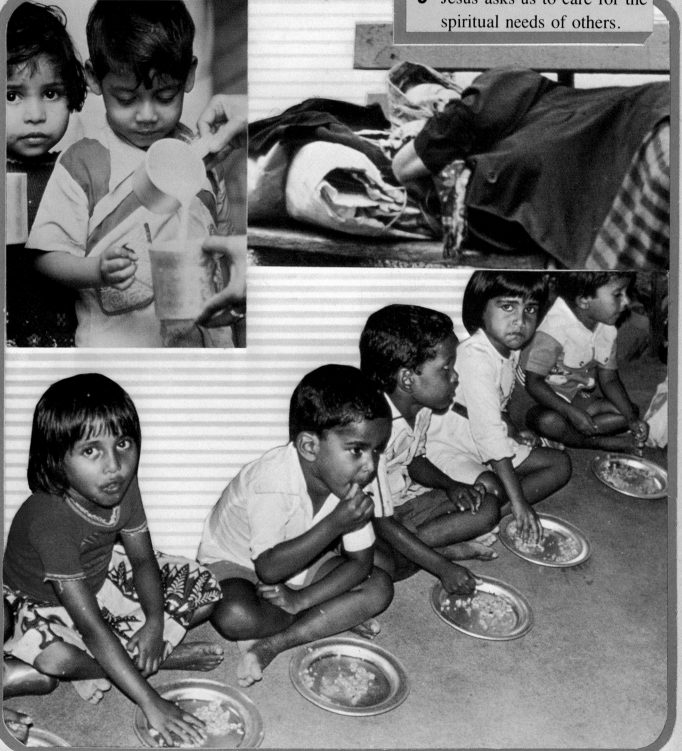

1 Jesus tells us about the Last Judgment.

Jesus told this story of how we should treat those in need, and why.

At the end of the world, on the last day, Jesus will come to judge all people. This is called the *Last Judgment*. To the just He will say: "Come you, that are blessed by My Father! . . ." Then He will surprise them by telling them why they are blessed. "I was hungry . . . and thirsty . . . a stranger . . . naked . . . sick . . . and in prison" and you helped Me and cared for Me."

And the just people will ask Jesus when they ever saw Him hungry, thirsty, and in such need. Jesus answers with the remarkable words: "Whenever you did this for one of the least important of these brothers and sisters of Mine, you did it for Me" (from Matthew 25:34–40). Jesus used this story to show us how to love others as members of God's Kingdom.

According to Jesus, when do we ever see Him in need?

Where do you see Jesus today?

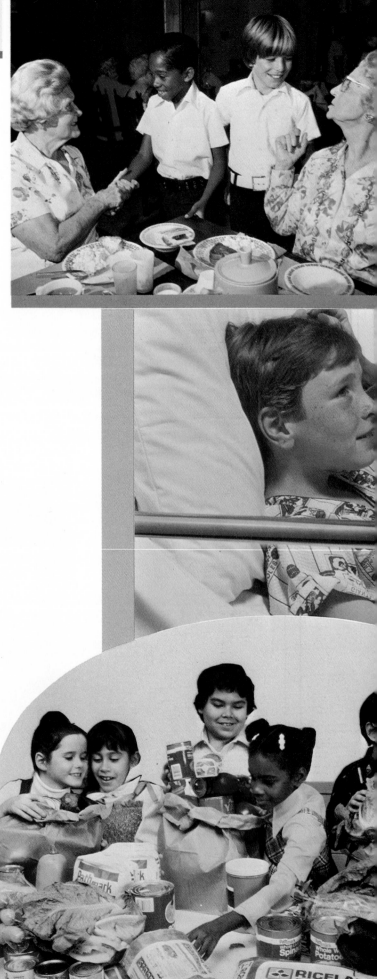

2 Jesus asks us to care for the physical needs of others.

All Christians are called to be just, peaceful, and loving as Jesus was. We are to carry on the *Corporal Works of Mercy* as Jesus asks:

- Feed the hungry.
- Give drink to the thirsty.
- Shelter the homeless.
- Clothe the naked.
- Care for the sick.
- Help those imprisoned.
- Bury the dead.

This is how we can make God's Kingdom real for all people everywhere.

Which of these Corporal Works of Mercy can people your age do? How?

Do You Know

As Catholics, we believe that death does not totally and finally separate the living from those who have died. We are all still brothers and sisters in Christ. We can still pray for one another. We call this union of all God's friends—living and dead—the *Communion of Saints*.

3 Jesus asks us to care for the spiritual needs of others.

We are more than just our bodies. We also have spirits which have their own needs. The *Spiritual Works of Mercy*, given to us by the Church, teach us to be patient, kind, understanding, and forgiving. They are:

- Teach the ignorant.
- Give advice to those who need it.
- Comfort those who are suffering.
- Be patient with others.
- Forgive those who hurt you.
- Give correction to those who need it.
- Pray for others.

The Spiritual Works also show us how we can make God's Kingdom real for all people everywhere.

Jesus asks us to practice the Spiritual Works of Mercy in our everyday lives so everyone will come to live more like Him.

Which of these Spiritual Works of Mercy can people your age do? How?

I Have Learned

Name the Corporal and Spiritual Works of Mercy. In your own words explain what they mean.

I Will Do

Think of possible slogans to encourage people to do the Works of Mercy.

Choose one, and design a bumper sticker for a car or bike. Make copies for your family or friends.

Which slogan will you try to live this week? this year?

Prayer

Let us pray a prayer of praise to the three Persons of the Blessed Trinity.

Glory to the Father,
and to the Son,
and to the Holy Spirit.
As it was in the beginning,
is now, and will be forever.
Amen.

Remember

Jesus teaches us that whatever we do to others we do to Him.

The Church teaches us how we can serve Jesus in doing the Corporal and Spiritual Works of Mercy.

Review

1. What do we mean by the Last Judgment?

2. Why should the Corporal and Spiritual Works of Mercy be important for you?

3. Do you find surprising the way Jesus says we will be judged? Why?

Family Note

This lesson focuses on the way we should live as Catholics, doing the Works of Mercy.

Share with your child your own thoughts and feelings about the importance of the Works of Mercy.

Faith Words

rosary:

a traditional prayer to Mary.

saint:

someone the Church honors as a faithful follower of Jesus.

Faithful Friends

Ben had come over to Lisa's house for some help with his English assignment. His teacher, Mrs. Crockett, had warned them that there would be an important grammar test in ten days.

While Lisa got them some juice out of the refrigerator, Ben looked at the calendar to see when the test was scheduled.

"Hey, Lisa, how come your calendar has all these names printed on it?" he asked.

"Those are the names of our saints," Lisa replied.

"But why are they on your calendar?" Ben asked.

Lisa explained that the Catholic Church honors many of its saints by celebrating their feast days.

"My mother says it's a nice way to remember our ancestors in God's family," Lisa said. "Isn't that right, Mom?"

"Yes," Lisa's mother answered. "The saints are our friends. They help us and pray for us. That's why parents often name their children after them. We named Lisa after St. Elizabeth."

Do you have a saint's name?

What do you know about your saint?

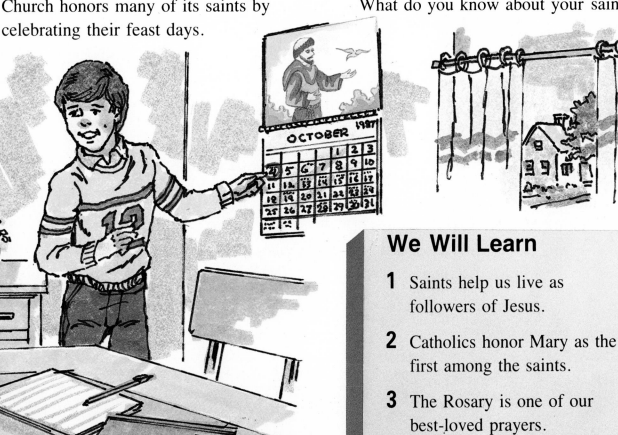

We Will Learn

1 Saints help us live as followers of Jesus.

2 Catholics honor Mary as the first among the saints.

3 The Rosary is one of our best-loved prayers.

1 Saints help us live as followers of Jesus.

Saints are holy people who tried to follow Jesus with all their hearts. The saints are our brothers and sisters in the Church. From heaven they continue to watch over and pray for the Church, for all of us. As Catholics, we remember and honor the saints because they show us how we, too, can follow Jesus with all our hearts.

No two saints are exactly alike. Saints have been men and women, and children. Some were married, some not; some were members of religious orders; some were lay people, some ordained. Saints have come from all parts of the world, from every age, and from all walks of life. Martin of Tours, for example, was a soldier, Elizabeth of Hungary a queen. There were lawyers like Thomas More, and poor people like Francis of Assisi and Clare. There were teachers like Mother Seton, missionaries like Peter Claver, and martyrs like Agnes.

Do you know any stories from the lives of the saints? Share one story.

What do the stories tell you about being a faithful follower of Jesus?

2 Catholics honor Mary as first among the saints.

As Catholics, we honor Mary as the greatest of the saints, because she is the mother of Jesus. Here are some things the Church teaches about Mary.

Mary was a young Jewish girl who had been brought up in the faith of her people. When the time came for the Savior to come, as God had promised, God chose Mary to be the mother of Jesus, God's own Son.

God's messenger came to Mary and said, ''You will become pregnant and give birth to a son, and you will name Him Jesus.''

Do You Know

Many times throughout the year we celebrate our love for Mary. Here are some of them.

Mary, the Mother of God —January 1
The Annunciation—March 25
The Visitation—May 31
The Assumption—August 15
The Birth of Mary—September 8
The Immaculate Conception— December 8

Mary was troubled by these words for she was a virgin and not yet married. God promised Mary that the Holy Spirit would come upon her and that her child would be the Son of God.

Mary believed and trusted in God's Word. She said, ''I am the servant of the Lord. Let what you have said happen to me'' (from Luke 1:26–38).

Mary became the virgin mother of Jesus Christ, God's Son. She loved and cared for Jesus all through His life.

The Gospel of John tells us that when Jesus was dying on the cross His Mother was there.

Many of His followers ran away and hid in fear, but Mary stayed with Jesus until the very end.

Jesus saw His mother and His friend John standing near the cross. He said to Mary, ''He is your son.'' Then he said to John, ''This is your mother.'' (John 19:25–27).

The Church tells us that by these words Jesus gave Mary to the whole Church to be the mother of us all.

Why do you think Mary is so important to the Church?

What does Mary mean to you?

3 The Rosary is one of our best-loved prayers.

One of the ways in which Catholics have shown honor to Mary is through the *rosary*. The rosary is a prayer in which we recall major events in the lives of Jesus and Mary. We begin the rosary with the Apostles' Creed (see page 106). The rosary is divided into five groups of ten beads with a single bead set before each group. Each group is called a *decade*. There is also a crucifix and four beads at the beginning of the rosary.

For each decade, we imagine one event or mystery from the lives of Jesus and Mary. Then we pray one Our Father, ten Hail Marys, and one Glory to the Father. (See text page 96 for a list of the mysteries of the rosary.)

Explain how to pray one decade of the rosary.

How might the rosary be helpful to you?

Mary and the saints show us that whoever we are and whatever we do in life, we, too, can be faithful followers of Jesus.

I Have Learned

Complete the following statements on Mary and the saints.

■ Catholics honor Mary because

_____ .

■ When we pray the rosary, we think about

_____ .

■ To me, a saint is someone who

_____ .

I Will Do

If you do not have a rosary, ask your teacher or parent where you can get one. Spend a few minutes picturing a favorite scene from the life of Jesus and Mary—the birth of Jesus, for example. Then say one decade of the rosary.

Prayer

This is one of the oldest and best loved prayers to Mary.

Hail Mary, full of grace
the Lord is with you;
blessed are you among women,
and blessed is the fruit
of your womb, Jesus.
Holy Mary, Mother of God,
pray for us sinners now
and at the hour of our death.
Amen.

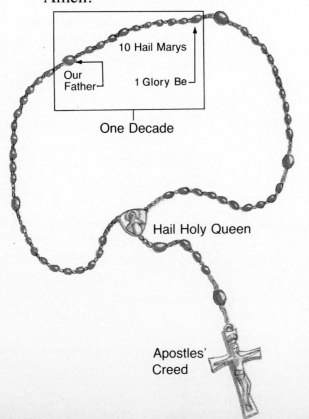

10 Hail Marys

Our Father

1 Glory Be

One Decade

Hail Holy Queen

Apostles' Creed

Remember

Catholics honor Mary as first among all the saints.

The saints show us how we can be faithful followers of Jesus.

Review

1. What do we admire in Mary?

2. Why do we honor the saints?

3. What will you do this week to become better acquainted with Mary or one of the other saints?

Family Note

This lesson focused on Catholic devotion to Mary and the saints. Your child learned that we look to Mary as the mother of Jesus and the model of our spiritual lives.

You might give your child a rosary or a picture of a particular saint he or she would like to know more about.

Unit IV Test

Write the word from this list that best fits each numbered description. One is done for you.

absolution
conscience
Beatitudes
Corporal Works
  of Mercy
Law of Love

rosary
Spiritual Works
  of Mercy
saint
Ten Commandments
sin

1. The basic laws of God

   _____

2. Someone the Church honors as a faithful follower of Jesus

   _____saint_____

3. Ways we can help those who suffer physically

   _____

4. Traditional prayer to Mary

   _____

5. Freely choosing to do something that we know is wrong

   _____

6. Love of God and neighbor

   _____

7. Jesus' guidelines for true happiness

   _____

8. The ability to know right from wrong

   _____

9. Ways we can help those who suffer in mind, heart, or spirit

   _____

10. A sign of God's forgiveness

   _____

11. What is the Law of Love?

   _____

   _____

Complete the following quotations with words from the Word List. After each quotation, write who said it.

name   Me
Kingdom of God   least important
Mine   birth
neighbor   covenant
chosen   yourself
all   care

11. "If you will obey me and keep my

_____ you will be my own

people, my _____ people."

_____

12. "You will give _____ to a son,

and you will _____ Him Jesus."

_____

13. "Love your _____ as _____ ."

_____

14. "Be concerned above everything else

with the _____ and God will take

_____ of _____ the rest."

_____

15. "Whenever you did this for one

of the _____ of these brothers

and sisters of _____ , you did

it for _____ ."

_____

Answer briefly the questions on the lines provided.

16. What do the first three commandments tell us?

_____

17. To help us live as true followers of Jesus, what are the three gifts God gives us?

_____

18. What are the two ways of celebrating the sacrament of Reconciliation?

_____

19. What is the name of the union of all God's friends, living and dead?

_____

20. Think first. Then answer this question. For you, what is the most important part of the sacrament of Reconciliation?

_____

_____

Second Semester Test

Circle the correct answer.

1. Each person who wishes to join the Catholic Church
   a. must have Catholic parents.
   b. must be a Christian.
   c. is welcomed through Baptism.
   d. must take a blood test.

2. After the death and resurrection of Jesus, His friends often met together to
   a. cry.
   b. pray and remember what Jesus said.
   c. plan a protest march.
   d. make a list of new Christians.

3. After we hear the readings from the Bible, the priest or deacon
   a. tells us to leave.
   b. asks us questions.
   c. asks if we heard him.
   d. explains the readings.

4. When we examine our conscience before Reconciliation, we
   a. plan how to hurt those who have hurt us.
   b. ask ourselves if we have loved God, others, and ourselves.
   c. know we are good.
   d. fast for 12 hours.

5. The first three commandments tell us
   a. how bad we are.
   b. how to make friends.
   c. how to love God.
   d. when to sing during Mass.

6. The other commandments tell us
   a. to read the Bible daily.
   b. how to love others.
   c. how to pray the rosary.
   d. how to live a long life.

7. We form our conscience by
   a. copying what our parents do.
   b. following our best friend's advice.
   c. learning to make decisions about right and wrong.
   d. reading a good story.

8. The Beatitudes are guidelines for
   a. true happiness.
   b. good health.
   c. non-believers.
   d. priests and deacons only.

9. The Corporal Works of Mercy are
   a. what the priest says at the end of Mass.
   b. things our parents make us do at home.
   c. prayers for the dead.
   d. ways we can help those who suffer physically.

10. The rosary is
    a. a stained-glass window.
    b. a prayer through which Catholics honor Mary.
    c. a flower arrangement
    d. a small chapel.

From the list of words below, write in the word or phrase that best complete each sentence. One is done for you.

Mass	Spiritual	life
temptation	saints	forgiving
God	God's	thanks
must do	happiness	Sunday
way	people	sin
prayer	give in	follow
frees	holy	

11. Baptism _____ us from _____ and gives us God's _____ .

12. The Mass is our great _____ of praise and _____ to _____ .

13. A sign of God's forgiveness is _____ .

14. Beatitude is a word that means "_____ to _____ ."

15. The Commandments tell us what we _____ _____ to be _____ _____ .

16. A _____ is not a sin unless we _____ _____ to it and do what is _____ .

17. The _____Spiritual_____ Works of Mercy teach us to be patient, kind, understanding, and _____forgiving_____ .

18. _____ are holy people who try to _____ Jesus.

19. Tell the steps in the sacrament of Reconciliation.

_____

_____

_____

20. Think first. Then answer this question. Jesus said, "Come, follow Me." As a believing Catholic, how are you doing this? (Use another piece of paper to answer this.)

101

A Review of the Year

1. **What is the Catholic Church?**
   The Catholic Church is the community of Christians who become followers of Jesus Christ through Baptism and who believe in the seven sacraments and in the leadership and authority of the pope and bishops.

2. **What is prayer?**
   Prayer is talking and listening to God.

3. **Name the three Persons of the Holy Trinity.**
   The three Persons of the Holy Trinity are God the Father, God the Son, and God the Holy Spirit.

4. **What is original sin?**
   Original sin is the first sin of humankind. All of us suffer the effects of this sin.

5. **Who is our Savior?**
   Jesus Christ, the Son of God, who saved us from sin and death is our Savior.

6. **What does the word *Incarnation* mean?**
   Incarnation is the word used to describe God becoming one of us in Jesus Christ.

7. **What does the word *Gospel* mean?**
   Gospel is a word that means good news.

8. **What happened on Holy Thursday?**
   On Holy Thursday Jesus shared His Last Supper with His friends. At that supper Jesus changed bread and wine into His Body and Blood.

9. **Why did Jesus suffer and die and rise again to new life?**
   Jesus suffered and died to give us God's own life so that we could live now with the help of God's grace and be happy with God forever in heaven.

10. **Who were the Apostles?**
    The Apostles were a special group of twelve men chosen by Jesus to lead His community.

11. **What happened on the feast of Pentecost?**
    The Holy Spirit came to the disciples in a special way.

12. **What are the Marks of the Church?**
    The Marks of the Church are *one*, *holy*, *catholic*, and *apostolic*.

13. **Who was the first pope and leader of the Catholic Church?**
    St. Peter was the first pope and leader of the Church.

14. What is a sacrament?
A sacrament is a life-giving sign given us by Christ through which we share God's life of grace.

15. What is the sacrament of Baptism?
Baptism is the sacrament through which new members are freed from original sin, welcomed into the Church, and begin to share God's own life of grace.

16. What is the sacrament of Confirmation?
Confirmation is the sacrament through which the Holy Spirit gives us the courage and strength to be witnesses to our faith.

17. What is the Holy Eucharist?
The Eucharist is the sacrament through which we are nourished by the Body and Blood of Jesus.

18. What is Holy Communion?
Holy Communion is the gift of Jesus Himself under the appearances of bread and wine.

19. What is the Mass?
The Mass is our celebration of the sacrament of the Eucharist when we worship God together with our parish community.

20. What are the Ten Commandments?
The Ten Commandments are laws God gave us to help us live as God's people.

21. What are the Beatitudes?
The Beatitudes are guidelines for true happiness taught by Jesus to His community.

22. What is the sacrament of Reconciliation?
The sacrament of Reconciliation is a life-giving sign of God's love and forgiveness in the Catholic Church.

23. What is sin?
Sin is a free choice to do something we know is wrong; something that damages our relationship with God.

24. What are the Corporal Works of Mercy?
The Corporal Works of Mercy are ways we care for one another's physical needs.

25. What are the Spiritual Works of Mercy?
The Spiritual Works of Mercy are ways we care for one another's minds and hearts.

26. Who is Mary?
Mary is the Virgin mother of Jesus Christ, God's Son.

The Liturgical Year

The seasons of the liturgical year are called Advent, Christmas, Lent, Easter, and Ordinary Time. Each season helps us to remember something about the life of Jesus.

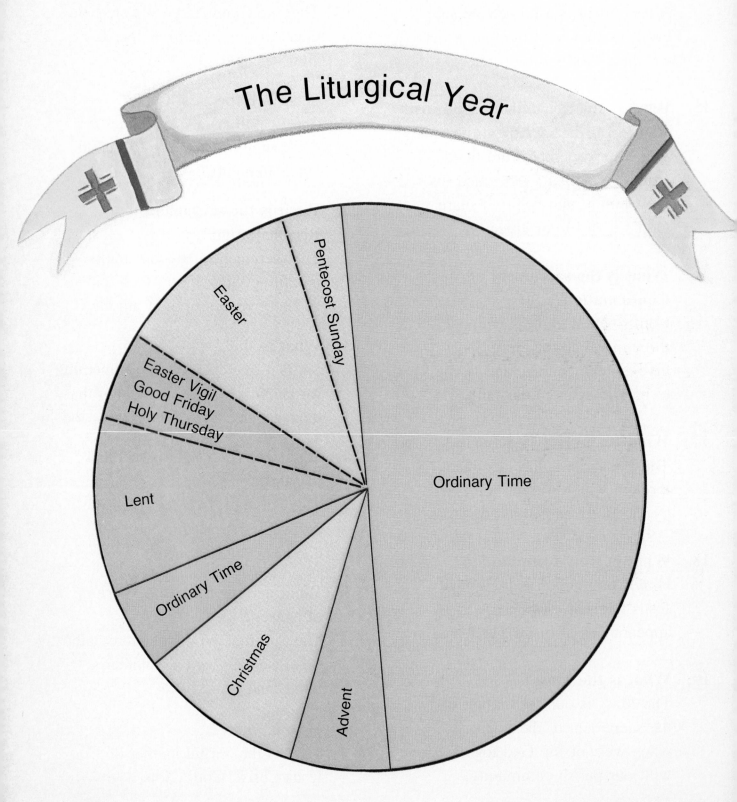

The Liturgical Year

Pentecost Sunday

Easter

Easter Vigil
Good Friday
Holy Thursday

Lent

Ordinary Time

Christmas

Advent

Ordinary Time

Advent

Advent is a time of preparation for Christmas. We recall the long years when God prepared the world for the birth of Jesus.

The Advent season begins four Sundays before December 25, and ends at the Christmas vigil Mass. The color of the vestments that the priest wears at this time is violet.

Christmas

Christmas is a time of great joy and love. We celebrate the birthday of Jesus, the Son of God.

The Christmas season begins at the vigil Mass on Christmas Eve and ends on the feast of the Baptism of the Lord. The color of the vestments for this season is white. You may also see gold vestments at this time. The joyous color symbolizes our joy at the birth of Jesus.

Lent

Lent is a time when we get ready for Easter. During Lent we try to come closer to Jesus by special prayers and acts of service to our family and other people. It is also a good time to celebrate the sacrament of Reconciliation.

The season of Lent begins on Ash Wednesday, 40 days before Easter, and ends just before the Holy Thursday liturgy. Once again the color of the priest's vestments at this time is violet.

Easter

The time between the end of Lent and Easter Sunday is called the Easter Triduum. This is a period of three very important days to Catholics: Holy Thursday, Good Friday, and the Easter Vigil. This is the most important time of the Church year. We rejoice as we remember that God raised Jesus from the dead and sent the Holy Spirit to guide the Church.

The Easter season begins on Easter Sunday and ends on Pentecost Sunday. The color of the priest's vestments is white or gold. Both of these colors signify the joy of the season of Resurrection.

Ordinary Time

All of the other Sundays throughout the year are called Ordinary Time. During Ordinary Time, the readings usually follow a pattern set by a particular Gospel. This is done to help us understand more about our faith and the story of salvation. The liturgical color for Ordinary Time is green, the color of hope.

Prayer

Our Father See page 65.

Hail Mary See page 97.

Glory to the Father See page 91.

Act of Contrition See page 85.

This is another Act of Contrition
suggested in the Rite of Reconciliation.

My God,
I am sorry for my sins with all my heart.
In choosing to do wrong
and failing to do good,
I have sinned against you
whom I should love above all things
I firmly intend, with your help,
to do penance, to sin no more,
and to avoid whatever leads me to sin.
Our Savior Jesus Christ
suffered and died for us.
In his name, my God, have mercy.

The Apostles' Creed

I believe in God, the Father Almighty,
   Creator of heaven and earth.

I believe in Jesus Christ, His only Son, our Lord.
   He was conceived by the power of the
      Holy Spirit
   and born of the Virgin Mary.
   He suffered under Pontius Pilate,
      was crucified, died, and was buried.
   He descended to the dead.
   On the third day He rose again.
   He ascended into heaven,
      and is seated at the right hand of the Father.
   He will come again to judge the
      living and the dead.

I believe in the Holy Spirit,
   the holy catholic Church,
   the communion of saints,
   the forgiveness of sins,
   the resurrection of the body,
   and the life everlasting. Amen

Sign of the Cross See page 31.

Hail, Holy Queen

Hail, Holy Queen, Mother of Mercy,
our life, our sweetness,
and our hope! To you do we cry,
poor banished children of Eve;
to you do we send up our sighs,
mourning and weeping in this
valley of tears. Turn, then,
most gracious advocate,
your eyes of mercy toward us,
and after this our exile,
show us the blessed
fruit of your womb, Jesus.
O clement, O loving,
O sweet Virgin Mary!

Praying the Rosary

The Joyful Mysteries:
- Mary agrees to become the Mother of Jesus.
- Mary visits her cousin Elizabeth.
- Jesus is born in Bethlehem.
- Jesus is presented in the Temple at Jerusalem.
- Mary and Joseph find Jesus in the Temple.

The Sorrowful Mysteries:
- Jesus suffers and prays in the garden.
- He is scourged at the pillar.
- He is crowned with thorns.
- He carries His cross.
- He is crucified and dies.

The Glorious Mysteries:
- Jesus rises to new life. This is the greatest event of all!
- Jesus returns to His Father in heaven.
- The Holy Spirit comes.
- Mary is taken to heaven, where she is with Jesus forever.
- Mary is crowned Queen and Mother of heaven and earth.

Glossary

Absolution: A sign that God forgives us through the actions and words of the priest in the sacrament of Reconciliation.

Apostles: A special group of twelve of Jesus' friends chosen by Him to lead His Church.

Baptism: The sacrament through which we are freed from original sin, welcomed into the Church, and begin to share God's own life of grace.

Beatitudes: Guidelines for true happiness taught by Jesus.

Bible: The book which tells the story of how God created us, loves us, and came among us.

bishop: A successor to the Apostles in teaching, serving, and leading the Church.

Blessed Trinity: The three divine Persons in one God: the Father, the Son, and the Holy Spirit.

Catholic Church: The community of Christians who become followers of Jesus Christ through Baptism and who believe in the seven sacraments and in the leadership and authority of the pope and bishops.

communion of saints: The union of all God's friends, living and dead.

Confirmation: The sacrament through which the Holy Spirit gives us the courage and strength to be witnesses to our faith.

conscience: The ability to know what is right or wrong, what we should or should not do.

Corporal Works of Mercy: Ways we show our love for others by helping those who suffer physically.

Creator: A name for God who created or made our universe and everything in it.

crucifix: A cross with the body of Jesus on it.

diocese: A group of parishes that has a bishop as its leader.

disciple: A friend and follower of Jesus.

Easter Sunday: The day Jesus rose from death to new life.

eternal life: Life that will last forever.

Eucharist: The sacrament of the Body and Blood of Jesus Christ.

examination of conscience: Thinking about the times when we sinned and failed to love God, others, or ourselves.

forming our conscience: Learning to make decisions about right and wrong.

gifts of the Holy Spirit

Wisdom—Being aware of God present in the world around us.

Courage—Living firmly by our Catholic faith.

Understanding—Having a deeper awareness of our Catholic faith.

Counsel—Being able to make good judgments in living.

Knowledge—Learning what is needed to serve God.

Reverence for God—Being devoted to God in all we do or say.

Piety—Being committed to a life of holiness.

Glossary

God the Father: The first Person of the Blessed Trinity.

God the Holy Spirit: The third Person of the Blessed Trinity who guides and helps the Church.

God the Son: The second Person of the Blessed Trinity.

Good Friday: The day Jesus died.

Gospel: The Good News of God's love for us.

gospels: The four books of the Bible that describe the life and teachings of Jesus.

grace: The gift of God's own life.

Holy Week: The week during which we remember the suffering, death, and resurrection of Jesus. It begins on Palm Sunday and ends on Easter.

Holy Communion: Receiving the gift of Jesus in the Eucharist under the appearances of bread and wine.

Holy Thursday: The day on which Jesus shared His Last Supper with His disciples and instituted the Holy Eucharist.

Holy Trinity: Three Persons in one God— Father, Son, and Holy Spirit.

Incarnation: God's only Son becoming a member of our human family in Jesus Christ.

justice: Being fair and concerned for the needs of all people.

Kingdom of God: The power of God's love, peace, and justice in the world.

Last Judgment: When Jesus will judge all the nations on the last day.

Last Supper: The last meal Jesus shared with His disciples before His death.

liturgy: The way we worship God in the Catholic Church.

marks of the Church: One, holy, catholic, apostolic; distinguishing traits or characteristics of the Catholic Church.

Mary: The mother of Jesus and model of a faithful follower of Jesus.

Mass: Our celebration of the sacrament of the Eucharist when we worship God together.

mortal sin: Very serious sin that destroys our friendship with God.

original sin: The first sin of humankind. All of us suffer from the effects of this sin.

parish: A community of Catholics, led by a pastor.

penance: A way for us to show that we are sorry for our sins.

Pentecost: The day the Holy Spirit came to the disciples.

pope: The successor to St. Peter as the bishop of Rome and leader of the Church.

priest: A man ordained by a bishop to preach the gospel, care for the parish's members, and celebrate the sacraments.

Reconciliation: The sacrament or life-giving sign of God's love and forgiveness in the Catholic Church.

Resurrection: Jesus' rising from death to new life.

rosary: A traditional prayer to Mary made up of at least five decades. In each decade we pray the Our Father and ten Hail Marys.

sacrament: A life-giving sign of God's grace given to the Church by Christ. There are seven sacraments.

saint: Someone the Church honors as a faithful follower of Jesus who is with Him in heaven.

salvation: The way in which we were freed from sin and death by the life, death, and rising of Jesus Christ.

Savior: Jesus, the Son of God, who saved us from sin and death.

sign: Something we can see, hear, touch, or taste that stands for something else.

sin: Freely choosing to do something we know is wrong and against God's will.

Spiritual Works of Mercy: Ways we show our love for others who suffer in mind, heart, or spirit.

temptation: A desire to do something wrong.

Ten Commandments: The basic laws of God that help us live together in freedom, justice, and peace.

venial sin: Less serious sin that weakens our friendship with God.

worship: Praise and adoration given to God.

Things to Know

The Church asks you to:

- Learn about Jesus and follow Him.

- Pray every day.

- Go to Mass on Sundays and Holy Days of Obligation to give praise and thanks to God. This shows how happy you are to be a member of the Catholic Church.

- Celebrate the sacrament of Reconciliation.

- Learn and live the teachings of our Catholic faith.

- Help your pastor and others who work in your parish.

Index

absolution, 83

Act of Contrition, 83

Adam and Eve, 8-10

Anointing:
   in Baptism, 50
   in Confirmation, 52

Anointing of the Sick, sacrament
   of, 41

Apostles, 15
   as foundation of the Church, 15
   at Pentecost, 28-29
   Resurrection appearances to,
      21-22

Ascension, 28

Baptism, 30, 41, 50-51
   effects of, 51
   Holy Spirit and, 30, 50
   initiation into the Church by,
      50, 52
   liturgy of, 50
   new life, 41
   original sin and, 51
   as sacrament of Initiation,
      50, 52
   as sign of unity, 50, 52

Beatitudes, 76-78
   list of, 77
   meaning of, 76-77
   purpose of, 78
   as way to true happiness, 78

Bible, 8-9, 14
   as God's holy Word, 62
   knowledge of God through, 62

Bishops, 35-36
   authority of, 36
   as leaders, 36
   as successors of Apostles, 36

Blessed Trinity, 26, 50

Church, 15, 29-30, 34-36
   leadership of, 36
   origins of, 15
   sacraments of, 40-41

Christmas, 14

Church, marks of:
   one, 35
   holy, 35
   catholic, 35
   apostolic, 35

Communion of Saints, 89

Confirmation, 41, 52
   Holy Spirit and, 52
   sign used in, 41, 52

Conscience, 82-84
   examination of, 82-84
   formation of, 82

Consecration of the Mass, 63

Corporal Works of Mercy, 89

covenant, 70

Creation, 8-9
   biblical account of, 8-9
   as gift of God, 9
   goodness and wonder of, 8-9
   of humankind, 8

Death and suffering of Jesus,
   20-22

Diocese, 36

Easter Sunday, 18, 21

Eighth Commandment, 71-72

Eucharist, sacrament of, 20, 41,
      56-58, 62, 63
   as Body and Blood of Christ,
      20, 56-58, 63
   as parish celebration, 57, 58
   as meal, 58, 63
   as memorial, 20, 56, 58
   as nourishment, 20, 56
   origins of, 20
   receiving the, 57-58
   as sacrament of Initiation, 50
   as sacrifice, 58
   Sunday observance of, 57

Examination of Conscience, 82-84

Faith, 78

Fifth Commandment, 71, 72

Forgiveness, 40, 41, 83-84. *See
   also* Reconciliation,
   sacrament of

Fourth Commandment, 71, 72

Gifts of the Holy Spirit, 52

God:
   as Creator and Lifegiver, 8-10
   as Father, 50
   respect/reverence for, 70,
      71, 72
   as Trinity, 26, 50

Good News of Jesus, 15-16

Good Friday, 18, 21

Gospel(s), 14-15

Grace, 41, 42, 51
   sacraments and, 41, 42

Holy Communion, 54, 56-58, 63
   ways of receiving, 63

Holy Orders, sacrament of, 41

Holy Spirit, 26, 28-30
   Baptism and, 30, 50
   Confirmation and, 52
   as Helper and Guide, 28
   on Pentecost, 28-30
   presence of, in Church, 30,
      35, 36
   promise/sending of, 28

Holy Thursday, 18, 20

Holy Week, 22

Incarnation, 12, 14

Jesus Christ, 10, 14-16, 56-58
  ascension of, 28
  birth of, 14
  death of, 21
  divinity of, 21-22, 28
  as gift of God, 10
  humanity of, 14
  incarnation of, 14
  mission of, 10, 15-16
  name of, respect for, 71, 72
  resurrection of, 21-22
  sacrifice of, 21
  signs of, 40

Jesus Christ, titles/descriptions of:
  Savior, 10, 16
  Son of God, 10, 14, 16
  Teacher, 15

Jesus Christ, mission of:
  to forgive sinners, 15, 22,
    40, 41
  to heal/comfort sick and
    suffering, 15, 40, 41
  to proclaim God's Kingdom, 16
  to serve poor, 15

Kingdom of God, 16, 89-90
  membership in, 16
  as work of God in the world,
    16, 34, 88-90

Kingdom values:
  love, peace, justice, 16

Last Judgment, 88

Last Supper, 20, 56, 57

Law of Love, 68, 71

Life, respect for, 71, 72

Liturgy, 60, 62

Liturgy of the Eucharist, 63

Liturgy of the Word, 62

Lord's Prayer, 63

Lying, 71, 72

Mary, 14, 94-95
  Annunciation, 14
  faith of, 95
  holiness of, 95
  Mother of Jesus, 14, 94-95
  virginity of, 95

Mass, 57, 60, 62-64. *See also*
  Eucharist

Mass, celebration of, 62-64

Matrimony, sacrament of, 41

Mortal sin, 82

Moses, 70

Ninth Commandment, 71, 72

Original sin, 8, 51

Parent(s), respect for, 71

Parish, 36

Passover, 56

Penance for sins, 83

Pentecost, 28-30

Peter, Saint, 15

Pope(s), 32, 36

Priests, 34, 36, 62, 63, 64

Reconciliation, sacrament of, 41,
  83-84
  effects of, 84
  elements of, 83
  rites of,
    communal, 84
    individual, 84

Resurrection of Jesus, 22
  appearances after, 21, 28
  Easter celebration of, 22
  effects of, 22

Rosary, 92, 96

Sabbath observance, 71, 72

Sacraments, 38, 40-42
  as life-giving signs, 42
  as signs of Jesus' presence,
    40, 42

Sacraments of Healing, 42

Sacraments of Initiation, 42, 50

Sacraments of Service, 42

Saints, 92, 94
  communion of, 89

Savior, promise of, 10

Second Commandment, 71, 72

Seventh Commandment, 71, 72

Sign, 38, 40

Sign of the Cross, 31

Sin, 80, 82
  mortal, 82
  original, 8, 51
  as turning away from God, 82
  venial, 82

Sixth Commandment, 71, 72

Spiritual Works of Mercy, 90

Stealing, 71, 72

Temptation, 82

Ten Commandments, 68, 70-72
  listing of, 71
  meaning of, 71, 72

Tenth Commandment, 71, 72

Third Commandment, 71, 72

Trinity, *See* Blessed Trinity

Venial sin, 82

Certificate of Achievement

(Your name)

has successfully completed this study of the basic beliefs of our Catholic faith.

(Your pastor or teacher)

(Date)

Photo Credits

The photographs reproduced on the pages listed are from the following sources:

Cover: John G. O'Connor left, R. Garcia right.

CARE 87 bottom, top right.
COMSTOCK: Tom Grill 7, 88; Judy Yoshioka 7.
John Fay 88-89 bottom.
Myrleen Ferguson 7, 30, 52-53, 54, 64, 75.
Ewing Galloway 7.
Ray Garcia 58, 87 top right, 89 bottom.
Robert Cushman Hayes 74.
Janet Charles 62.
Icon Communication/F.P.G. 9.
John Lei 20, 51, 63, 83.
Ed Lettau/F.P.G. 18-19.
Mark IV 48-49, 98.
Guy Marche/F.P.G. 12.
Maryknoll 17.
Mary Messenger 8, 12.
Mark Mittleman 21, 34, 83, 88 top, 95.
Donna Meier 53.
Metropolitan Museum of Art – Lehman Collection 56-57.
NASA 9.
Paul Robert Perry 12, 78, 86.
David Phillips 63 right.
Blair Seitz/F.P.G. 8.
Nancy Sheehan 83.
J. Gerald Smith 36.
Stock Solution: Doug Wilson 38 left.
Jeffrey Sylvester/F.P.G. 28-29.
Wes Thomas 58.
Vision Impact: Roger Smith 38 right.